Creative Groups Guide

Faith's Fundamentals

7
Complete
Lessons

Adapted for Group Study by Kent Odor and Mark Ingmire

STANDARD
PUBLISHING
Cincinnati, Ohio

Creative Groups Guide: Faith's Fundamentals

Adapted for Group Study by Kent Odor and Mark Ingmire

Edited by Michael C. Mack
Supplementary materials written by Michael C. Mack

All Scripture quotations, unless otherwise indicated, are taken from the *Holy Bible: New International Version*®. NIV®. Copyright © 1973, 1978, 1984 by International Bible Society. Used by permission of Zondervan Bible Publishers. All rights reserved.

Scripture quotations cited from the *Faith's Fundamentals* handbook are from the *New American Standard Bible*. © The Lockman Foundation 1960, 1963, 1968, 1971, 1972, 1973, 1975, 1977. Used by permission.

Cover design by Listenberger Design Associates.

The Standard Publishing Company, Cincinnati, Ohio.
A division of Standex International Corporation.

02 01 00 99 98 97 96 95   5 4 3 2 1

ISBN 0-7847-0391-4

$\mathcal{C}$ontents

oreword

Spiritual warfare is a topic that has received a lot of attention lately. This is good. We must never forget that "our struggle is not against flesh and blood, but against the rulers, against the powers, against the world forces of this darkness, against the spiritual forces of wickedness in the heavenly places" (Ephesians 6:12). These "spiritual forces" are Satan and his demons.

Each Christian is a personal target of Satan, marked for conquest. The devil's goal is to strip us of our saving faith in Christ. He is working hard to overthrow the church itself, to dilute its influence and to render it ineffective in its mission.

For a successful defense against deceitful spirits and doctrines of demons, it is not enough just to *have* the Word of God, in the sense of owning a Bible. It is not enough simply to know its contents, with Bible knowledge being only a mental exercise. It is not enough just to have a passive, implicit faith in its contents, or to say, "Sure, I believe whatever the Bible says."

Of course, we must know the teaching of God's Word, and we must believe it as truth. But we must also know that this truth is our only sure weapon against the deadly attacks of Satan, and we must love it (2 Thessalonians 2:10) and guard it and wield it boldly in our personal lives and in the church.

In this book, the existence and value of truth or sound doctrine are presupposed. My goal in *Faith's Fundamentals* is to identify and explain the essential core of Christian doctrine, the "point of the sword," so to speak. That other doctrines are not discussed does not imply their unimportance or irrelevance. Indeed, all Scripture is God-breathed and is therefore the one true measure for sound doctrine and holy living (see 2 Timothy 3:16, 17). But without the seven doctrines discussed here, all the rest is futile. To espouse a "Christianity" that does not include these truths is like putting on "armor" made of cardboard and carrying a rubber "sword."

May studying this book make you better equipped to stand firm against the deceiver. May you think of it as tightening your armor about you, and sharpening your sword.

—Jack Cottrell, *Faith's Fundamentals*

$\mathcal{I}$ntroduction

Welcome to Creative Groups Guides!

Whether your group meets in a classroom at the church building or in the family room in someone's home, this guide will help you get the most out of your session.

You can use this Creative Groups Guide with or without *Faith's Fundamentals,* the companion book written by Jack Cottrell. Use this guide even if you haven't read that book. But if you do read it, you'll be even more equipped for leading the group.

Each section in this guide includes two plans—one for classes and one for small groups. This gives the leader several options:

• Use the plan just as it is written. If you teach an adult Sunday school or an elective class, use Plan One. If you lead a small group, use Plan Two.

• Perhaps you teach a Sunday school class that prefers a small group style of teaching. Use the discussion questions in Plan Two, but don't overlook the great ideas presented in Plan One. Mix and match the two plans to suit your class.

• Use the best of both plans. Perhaps you could start off your class with a discussion activity in Plan Two, and then use the Bible-study section in Plan One. Use the accountability or memory verse options presented in Plan Two in your Sunday school class. Use some of the "Sunday school" activities and resource sheets presented in Plan One in your small group meeting. Variety is the spice of life!

Resource sheets are available in each session for you to tear out and photocopy for your class or group. Overhead transparency masters are also included for most sessions. Use your own creativity as you decide how to make these resources work for you.

This guide has been developed to help you do several things. First, you'll be able to *facilitate active and interactive learning.* These methods help students remember and put into practice what they learn. Second, you'll *help your class or group apply the lessons to their lives.* These sessions will help your group members actually do something with what they're studying. Third, we've given you *lots of options.* Only you know what will work best in your class or group. Finally, *support and encouragement* are integrated into each session. Learning and application happen best when participants are helping one another. That may mean accountability if your group has built up the trust and caring it takes, or it may simply mean that people are lovingly encouraging one another to continue growing in knowledge and action.

How to Use This Guide

Each session begins with an excerpt from *Faith's Fundamentals.* This excerpt summarizes the session at a glance. Use it in your preparation or read it to your class or group as an introduction to a session. The central theme and lesson aims help you understand the main ideas being presented and what outcomes you are looking for.

Materials you might need on hand to conduct your session are listed on the first page of each of the plans.

In both plans, there are three main parts to each session: *Building Community,* a warm-up activity or icebreaker question; *Considering Scripture,* Bible-study activities and discussion; and *Taking the Next Step,* activities or discussion that will help participants apply what they have learned.

In Plan One for classes, the names of activities are listed in the margins, along with the suggested time for each one. Use these to stay on track as you plan your lesson and as you teach. In most cases, optional activities are listed. Use these instead of or in addition to other activities as time allows.

In Plan Two for groups, a resource sheet with multiple-choice discussion questions is included for each session. Use these multiple-choice questions to stimulate conversation. There are no "right" answers, so everyone should be able to choose a response and then expand on it. Participants do not have to limit their responses to the choices offered—encourage them to share their own thoughts and ideas if they are not included in the choices. Ask follow-up questions such as "Why did you pick that response?" or "Tell me more," to draw more out of group members.

Several other options are included in Plan Two for groups. Use the accountability-partner option to help the group support, encourage, and hold one another accountable. This works particularly well in a group in which trust has already been gained among participants. Accountability partners can help one another put what they are learning each week into practice. An optional memory verse is also included. Use it at your discretion to help your group grow in hiding God's Word in their hearts.

Use this guide to help you prepare, but we suggest that you do not take this book to your class or group meeting and merely read from it. Instead, take notes on a separate sheet of paper and use that as you lead your group.

Fundamental #1

Truth Itself Is Fundamental

*H*olding to the reality of truth is difficult in the face of militant relativism, but for Christians it is absolutely fundamental. Unbelievers generally gravitate toward relativism, especially with regard to ultimate questions, since it enables them to justify their wicked behavior (Romans 1:21–32). The only viewpoint they will *not* tolerate is the belief in absolute and exclusive truth. Hence early Christians were persecuted not so much for believing in Jesus, but for believing that all other gods and religions are false. Likewise, modern Bible believers ("right-wing fundamentalists") are singled out for attack not for their faith as such, but because their commitment to absolute truth makes them intolerant of false worldviews and false lifestyles.

—Jack Cottrell, *Faith's Fundamentals*

Central Theme   Being a Christian makes a difference because Christianity is grounded in truth.

Lesson Aim   Learners will discover three things about truth:
- What truth is
- Why truth is important
- That truth is Jesus Christ

Bible Background   John 14:1–7; 18:33–37

For Further Study   Read the Introduction and Chapter One of *Faith's Fundamentals*.

Classes

BUILDING COMMUNITY

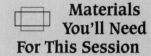 To open the class, use <u>Transparency 1A</u> or simply write the question from the transparency on the chalkboard: **"When it comes to telling the truth about current news events, whom do you trust the most? Why?"** Save space below the question to list the responses. Some responses might include: newspapers, television, Rush Limbaugh, Christian television, James Dobson, politicians.

After spending some time discussing the first question, take a few more minutes to follow it up by asking, **Why do you think there are such diverse views concerning what is true?** The bottom line to the class's responses could be summed up by Jack Cottrell's words: "In the end all that matters is what you *like* or *value."*

Close the "Building Community" time with these thoughts: **Current relativism says, "There is no such thing as absolute truth." If that statement is true, then it becomes absolute and the statement itself becomes false. However, the reality remains that for many people truth is simply what works for them at any one particular time, and it may be subject to change. In other words, the truth becomes relative.**

As disciples of Christ, who says we have the corner on truth? With so many different religions in the world, how do we know *we* are right? Wouldn't it make sense that all religions can lead us to God? It makes us ask the question: "Does it really matter that I am a Christian?"

CONSIDERING SCRIPTURE

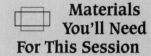 For the following exercise, divide the class into three groups. Hand out copies of <u>Resource Sheet 1A</u> to one group, copies of <u>Sheet 1B</u> to another group, and <u>1C</u> to the remaining group. As the sheets are being passed around, introduce the Bible study by sharing these thoughts with the class: **People claiming to have the inside track on the truth is nothing new. Even when Jesus walked the earth, people were as diverse as we are today concerning what is truth.**

Ask the members of each group to read the Scriptures listed on their sheets and discuss the questions that follow. After they have

What Is True?
15 Minutes

Materials You'll Need For This Session

Resource Sheets 1A–1D, a chalkboard and chalk or Transparency 1A and an erasable marker

Read and Discuss
25–30 Minutes

discussed the questions, they are to write a brief paragraph to answer the question that is also the title of their resource sheet. They should be prepared to share their responses with the class. Allow them twenty minutes to answer the questions. Then take five to ten minutes to let the groups share their paragraphs with the rest of the class.

Summary and Transition
5 Minutes

Close the "Considering Scripture" time with these thoughts: **Truth is fundamental to our lives. Without the truth, we would be like those Paul talked about in Ephesians 4:14, which says, "Then we will no longer be infants, tossed back and forth by the waves, and blown here and there by every wind of teaching and by the cunning and craftiness of men in their deceitful scheming." Being a Christian does make a difference. As Christians, we know the truth, and the truth is Jesus. But how can we apply this truth to our lives?**

TAKING THE NEXT STEP

On the Road to Truth
10 Minutes

Have the class come back together as one group. Once the class is settled, distribute <u>Resource Sheet 1D</u> and read the two paragraphs at the top of the sheet. Ask each person in the class to consider this statement: **"Jesus is the way to truth. The trip may be tough, but Jesus always gives us hope and life along the way."**

Determine where you are on this road by checking one of the choices. Have the class complete this multiple-choice question. After about a minute, ask if anyone would be willing to share where she thinks she is on the road to truth.

Words from Jesus
5 Minutes

Once there has been time for the students to share their responses, ask someone to read aloud the paragraph on the bottom half of <u>Resource Sheet 1D</u>. Then give the students several minutes to write a brief message as if it were to them from Jesus.

Ask a few people to share what words they think Jesus would say to them today. Once a few have shared, close in prayer, asking God to help participants in today's study pursue the truth who is Jesus.

PLAN TWO

Groups

BUILDING COMMUNITY

• Distribute copies of <u>Resource Sheet 1E</u> to participants. Begin the meeting with question 1 as an icebreaker.

• OPTION: Use the following activity either in addition to or in the place of question 1 on the resource sheet.

As a group, try to develop a simple definition of *truth* that a child could understand. (Encourage the group to picture in their minds a four- to six-year-old child. If anyone has a photograph of a child, have that person show the picture to the group as a visual aid.)

Then ask, **Why is truth important?**

CONSIDERING SCRIPTURE

Ask a volunteer (or several) to read aloud ***Psalms 25:4, 5; 26:2, 3; 31:5; 40:10, 11; and 43:3.* As you listen, pay special attention to what could be considered "some of the essentials" of truth.**

After the Scripture passages are read, discuss questions 2 and 3 on the resource sheet.

After discussing question 3, say, **In the first chapter of *Faith's Fundamentals,* Jack Cottrell establishes a case that, in our age, truth is under question. He says truth today is relativistic; that is, it is based on what an individual thinks it is to himself alone. Cottrell points out that it is the presence of error that makes truth become clear and helps us agree that it even exists. The fact that on a daily basis a newspaper will retract its mistakes is evidence that not everything is "true."**

Ask a volunteer to read ***John 18:33–38.* Then discuss questions 4 and 5 on the resource sheet.**

After discussing question 5, say, **Jesus cared about truth. He felt that truth mattered a great deal, and he is the link that connects all men to God. Just the evening before, while in the upper room with his disciples, he said, "I am the way and the truth and the life. No one comes to the Father except through me" (John 14:6). In this statement he declared both "what" truth is and "why" truth is important. He established a truth that matters—one that is essential for life.**

Then discuss questions 6 and 7 on the resource sheet.

Materials You'll Need For This Session

Resource Sheet 1E, Resource Sheet 1D for the accountability partner option

OPTION
Accountability Partners

Ask each participant in the group to pair up with another person, preferably not a spouse, with whom they will meet throughout this series. (Often they will meet at the end of a meeting, but they may also meet or talk on the telephone at other times during the week.)

Distribute Resource Sheet 1D to each person, and have the partners discuss the question together. When they finish, ask them to pray together to close this session.

OPTION
Memory Verse

"For this reason I was born, and for this I came into the world, to testify to the truth. Everyone on the side of truth listens to me" (John 18:37).

TAKING THE NEXT STEP

Read the following true story aloud. This story is about a missionary and his encounter with village people in an Asian country.

The missionary entered the village, and it caused a great commotion. The chief of the village was summoned. He welcomed the missionary and immediately ordered food and the best that village had to offer to be brought to his hut. The missionary learned that the village had already been evangelized and the people were already believers, and so there was much joy. As he talked with the chief, the missionary began to realize that the village had been expecting him to arrive for some time, which was unusual because he was not familiar with this village at all.

After a little while, the chief indicated that he wanted to show the missionary something important. He was led to a hut that was different from all the other huts in the village and seemed to have some special importance. As the chief proudly showed the contents of the hut to the missionary, he indicated that this was what the entire village had collected to be sent to the poor in Jerusalem.

The missionary was puzzled, so the chief referred to the message in "the book" that indicated that believers everywhere were collecting for the poor in Jerusalem and that soon someone would come and receive the offering and take it to those in need. It dawned on the missionary that the chief was referring to the famine relief recorded in Acts 11:27–30. The missionary began to explain that this request was from a long time ago and that the need had been met almost two thousand years before. The chief looked disheartened and astonished. He replied simply, "What took you so long to tell us?"

Though the timing of the collection mentioned in "the book" had not been understood, the essential truth of the gospel had been fully understood, and the people of the village had obediently put their faith and trust in Christ. The chief's question when applied to the central truth of the gospel still impacts us today.

Discuss questions 8 and 9 on the resource sheet to close the session.

WHAT IS TRUTH?

Read John 18:33–37 and the following quote from the **Faith's Fundamentals** *handbook. Then discuss the questions that follow.*

Accepting a statement or claim as true is a decision that is always grounded in sufficient reason or sufficient evidence. In general, this is done in two ways.

First, we accept some things as true because we have personally experienced them. We know fire is hot, because we have been burned by it. . . . Actually, only a small portion of what we regard as truth comes to us in this way.

Second, most of what we accept as true has come to us through the testimony of others. Technically speaking, all truth received in this way is a matter of *faith.* The data comes to us not through personal experience but through the reports of other, and we *believe* them.

What did Pilate mean when he said, "What is truth?"

Did Pilate have any reason to believe Jesus was telling the truth?

How could Pilate have determined the truth about Jesus?

From your discussion, write a paragraph describing what truth is.

WHY IS TRUTH IMPORTANT?

Read John 14:1–7 and the following quote from the* Faith's Fundamentals *handbook. Then discuss the questions that follow.

Probably the most pervasive characteristic of our modern culture is its abandonment of absolutes. "Truth" is relative to particular times, places, and people. What is true for you in your cultural context may be false for me in my situation. What is true for you today may be false for you to-morrow. . . .

If this view is *true* (note the inherent contradiction!), then it has the most drastic consequences. For example, history can be rewritten at will. Schools can abandon fact-oriented curricula and focus on behavior modi-fication. Teachers' views are no more "correct" than students'; parents' decisions are no more "right" than those of their children. No one's con-duct can be criticized; neither Hitler nor idol worshipers can be con-demned. When you are ill, it won't really matter what medicine you take.

What happens to us when we are lied to?

What are the consequences of knowing the truth?

How do Jesus' words in verses 1–7 give hope to the disciples?

How do Jesus' words give life to the disciples?

From your discussion, write a paragraph explaining why truth is important.

WHO IS THE TRUTH?

Read John 14:1–7 and the following quote from the **Faith's Fundamentals** *handbook. Then discuss the questions that follow.*

Holding to the reality of truth is difficult in the face of militant relativism, but for Christians it is absolutely fundamental. Unbelievers generally gravitate toward relativism, especially with regard to ultimate questions, since it enables them to justify their wicked behavior (Romans 1:21–32). The only viewpoint they will *not* tolerate is the belief in absolute and exclusive truth. Hence early Christians were persecuted not so much for believing in Jesus, but for believing that all other gods and religions are false.

Who does John 14:1–7 say is the truth?

What does it mean to be the truth?

Why do you believe Jesus when he says that he is the way, the truth, and the life?

From your discussion, write a paragraph describing who is the truth.

My Place on the Road to
TRUTH

Our pursuit of the truth can be compared to taking a trip to a place we long to go. We are excited about getting to our destination. Along the way, we may find ourselves lost, discouraged, frustrated, and without hope, but we may also find the trip to be fun, full of joy and laughter.

Jesus is the way to truth. The trip may be tough, but Jesus always gives us hope and life along the way.

Determine where you are on this road by checking one of the choices below.

❏ In the ditch

   ❏ Filling up the gas tank

      ❏ Lost but making good time

         ❏ In a traffic jam

            ❏ Wanting to ask directions

               ❏ Broken down on the side of the road

                  ❏ Traveling a smooth road

                     ❏ Hitting a few potholes

                        ❏ Other:

Everyone may be at a different spot on the road. What Jesus wants to share with you will be based on where you find yourself on that road. Consider the words of hope and life Jesus shared with his disciples in John 14; then write down the words of hope and life you think Jesus wants to share with you as you journey on the road to truth.

Dear_____ :

Your Way to Truth,

Jesus

Small Group Discussion

BUILDING COMMUNITY

1. Can you remember a time as a child or teenager when you were caught in a lie? Please briefly tell the story, answering these questions.
   - What was the lie?
   - Who was involved?
   - How did you feel before you were caught?
   - What did you do when caught?
   - How did the truth come out?
   - How did you feel afterward?

CONSIDERING SCRIPTURE

Psalms 25:4, 5; 26:2, 3; 31:5; 40:10, 11; 43:3

2. What do you think are the most essential properties of truth that can be seen in the words of these psalms?
   - a. Truth is like a path that a person can follow rather than wandering in any direction.
   - b. Truth is clearer when in the presence of the Lord.
   - c. Truth is part of the essence of God.
   - d. The truth of God is reflected through us when we receive it from him.
   - e. Truth is a protector of life.
   - f. Truth is a light on the path of life that will lead to the Father.

3. How can knowing that our God is truth help us in our everyday lives?
   - a. Words of truth are now closer to the source of truth.
   - b. Words of truth always bring us inner and mental strength.
   - c. People seem to continue growing and developing as they continue to absorb greater amounts of truth.
   - d. Words of truth from God always provide direction for the future.
   - e. Other.

John 18:33–38

4. What do you think Pilate's questions reflect about the condition of his own heart?
   - a. It doesn't really matter if Jesus is truth or not.
   - b. Truth is relative, not absolute.
   - c. He doesn't really want to know the whole truth; he just wants to know enough to get Jesus' case off his back.
   - d. He is most concerned about his own position and power.

5. What do you think is the greatest similarity between Pilate and many people in our day as they reflect on the question, "What is truth?"
   - a. They both wonder how important it is to really know the truth.
   - b. They think it is easier to be ignorant than to know the truth and then have to respond to it.
   - c. They desire to pass the buck rather than face the truth themselves.
   - d. They turn and run in the other direction.

John 14:6

6. What in Jesus' statement makes truth hard for us to accept?
   - a. Any "truth" other than Jesus misses the mark.
   - b. He is the only way to God.
   - c. Truth and life are connected; life without truth doesn't work.
   - d. *Jesus equals truth* is hard to comprehend. No one is perfect, right?

7. What impact could Jesus' words of truth have on the life of a man or woman who honestly considered them?
   - a. They could ask themselves, "Where am I going? Is Jesus the way for me?"
   - b. They could ask Jesus to show them the way so they could follow.
   - c. They might realize they have been walking in the wrong direction.
   - d. They might deal with whatever has hindered them from walking along the way of Christ.

TAKING THE NEXT STEP

8. What will it take for you to "not wait" to share the truth you have received in Jesus with someone you know who hasn't heard it?
   - a. A greater commitment to the lordship of Christ in my life
   - b. A deeper conviction that lost people matter to God
   - c. A deeper commitment to the absoluteness of the truth of God's Word
   - d. Encouragement from others to boldly advance

9. Is there something you can do to share "truth" with people so they never have to ask, "What took you so long to tell me?"
   - a. Pray for them
   - b. Befriend them
   - c. Meet a felt need in their life
   - d. Pass on to them a piece of "truthful" literature
   - e. Encourage them to seek the truth
   - f. Invite them to attend a program where the truth will be shared

Who Is Telling the Truth?

❖ ❖ ❖

When it comes to telling the truth about current news events, whom do you trust the most? Why?

Fundamental #2

God Is Real

*I*t is one thing to say that truth is fundamental; it is another thing to say that this or that particular idea is true. This applies especially to the truths that we would consider to be the most crucial.

We may indeed be convinced that there is such a thing as truth, contrary to the prevailing relativism. We may have the most sincere desire to possess that truth. But how? The humbling fact is this: It is impossible *only* if God exists. God alone is the foundation of the very concept of truth, and he is the sole source of the most vital truths sought by man.

So in a real sense, the most basic fundamental is the fact that God *exists.*

—Jack Cottrell, *Faith's Fundamentals*

Central Theme   God exists, and he alone is the foundation for all truth.

Lesson Aim   Learners will discover three things about God:
- Why truth can exist only if God exists
- What makes the God of Jesus Christ different from other gods
- Why it matters that we follow the God of Jesus Christ

Bible Background   Romans 1:18–25

For Further Study   Read Chapter Two of *Faith's Fundamentals.*

Classes

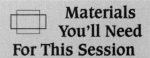

Materials You'll Need For This Session

Chalkboard, chalk, three boxes, wrapping paper, scissors, tape, Resource Sheets 2A–2C, and Transparency 2A

BUILDING COMMUNITY

As class members enter the room, ask one of them to be ready to read Romans 1:18–25.

Ask the class to divide into groups of four to six people each. In those groups have them discuss the following question: **When did God first become real to you?** Write the question on the chalkboard so they can refer to it as they spend the next few minutes talking about the question.

Small Group Discussion
10 Minutes

For this option you will need three boxes, wrapping paper, and wrapping tape. Before the class meets, find three boxes no larger than a shoe box. Find an object such as a ruler, pen, or can of food that can fit in one of the boxes. Place the object in the box so that it can move about freely and put wrapping paper around the box. Place a sheet of paper in the second box, and wrap up the box. Place nothing in box three, but simply wrap it up like boxes one and two.

OPTION
Guess What's Inside
10 Minutes

To begin class, pass around boxes one and two and ask each person to answer the following questions: **Is there something in the box? If so, why do you think so?** Then ask, **What do you think is in the box?** Write two headings on the chalkboard to list the class's responses. Title one heading, "Reasons Why" and the second, "Reasons What." Once the class members have exhausted their responses, ask someone to open the package to see how close the class guessed what was inside.

Now set box three someplace where the class can see it. Tell the class that you have wrapped up God in this box. Ask the class, **If I were able to put God in the box, how would you know he was actually in there?**

Close the "Building Community" time with these thoughts: **Throughout the ages, people have asked one simple but complex question: "Is God real?"**

How do we know that God exists? Sometimes it seems as if we have been handed a wrapped package without knowing if anything at all is inside. We can look at the size to rule out items that are larger than the package. We can lift the package to see how heavy it is, or we can shake it to find out what sound it makes. The only way we know for sure what is in the package is to open it. God is like the object in the box in the

sense that, while we live in a world that is seen, God is not seen by the human eye. Therefore, people may be given a package and told that God is inside, but even by looking, lifting, and shaking it they don't know if God is really there. In this lesson we will look into why God's existence is essential if truth is to exist. We will also look at what makes the God of Jesus Christ different from the gods of other religions.

Consider the Quote
10 Minutes

Pass around copies of <u>Resource Sheet 2A</u>. Ask someone from the class to read the excerpt from *Faith's Fundamentals* to the class. Then, using the quote, list as many reasons as you can that truth can only exist if God exists. Responses may include: man is finite, God is infinite; God knows all things, man is a created being; God is the Creator, not the created; God is the prototype for all reasoning. The point that this exercise makes is that absolute truth cannot exist unless God himself exists.

CONSIDERING SCRIPTURE

Read and Discuss
20 Minutes

Distribute copies of <u>Resource Sheet 2B</u>. With this short Bible study the class will continue to investigate the idea that truth can exist only if God exists. Ask your class to turn to Romans 1:18–25. Ask the designated person to read the passage at this time. Take about ten minutes to discuss each of the two sections.

Test Your Knowledge of World Religions
5 Minutes

What makes the God of Jesus Christ different from all other gods? Hand out <u>Resource Sheet 2C</u>. The answers to this exercise are below.

Hinduism—This eastern religion believes there is no existence of a personal God.

Islam—There is no God but Allah, and he is separated from the world.

Judaism—God is one and his people are still waiting for the Messiah.

Buddhism—Brahman takes form in millions of lesser gods.

New Age Movement—This popular movement inherited its roots from eastern religions.

Deism—God created the world, but he does not intervene into its history.

Jehovah's Witnesses—Jesus is a created being, and the doctrine of the Trinity is from Satan.

Mormonism—God was once as we are now and, like him, we can become a god.

(*NOTE: Hinduism and Buddhism have some similar features and may be difficult for students to differentiate without further study.*)

Close this exercise with these thoughts: **The difference between all other religions and Christianity begins with the doctrine of God. The errancy of doctrine in the world's religions can be traced to their doctrine about God. Therefore, it does matter which god we put our faith in. Without knowing the true God, it is impossible to know the truth. It does matter that we follow the God of Jesus Christ.**

TAKING THE NEXT STEP

Hand out copies of <u>Resource Sheet 2D</u>. Ask the class to review Romans 1:18–23 and to discuss the three questions on the sheet. After the class has answered question three, have each student pair up with another person. Instruct pairs to share their lists from question three with their partners and to pray for each other that they will follow through with their ideas. After the class has had time to pray with their partners, lead them in a closing prayer to close the class time.

Review and Discuss
15 Minutes

PLAN TWO roups

BUILDING COMMUNITY

What is the earliest memory you have about God?
- How was God "introduced" to you?
- What was your "impression" as best you can remember?

Why do you think some people have trouble believing in God?

CONSIDERING SCRIPTURE

Before the meeting, ask three volunteers to read the Scripture passages for this session *(Romans 1:18–32; Psalm 19:1–6; and Psalm 8:3–9)*. Begin the Bible study by saying, **Believing in God seems to be very difficult for many people today, especially those in the Western Hemisphere. In cultures that have given themselves to the pursuit of knowledge and reason, many individuals seem to have concluded that God is not necessary. Listen carefully as Romans 1:18–32 is read. This passage demonstrates that the existence of God is undeniable, and it presents a cause-and-effect situation that explains the problems seen in the societies of the whole world.**

Ask the selected person to read *Romans 1:18–32*. Then distribute a copy of Resource Sheet 2E to each participant. Discuss questions 1–5 for this first section of Scripture. Go around the circle and on each question let the next person to the right of the leader begin the sharing by answering first. Make sure each person shares why he selected his answer. After the first person shares, the rest of the group can discuss other insights, choices, and answers until it's time to move on to the next question.

After discussing question 5, say, **The Bible presents God's presence in nature strongly in the following Jewish songs written three thousand years ago.** Ask the volunteers to read *Psalm 19:1–6* and *Psalm 8:3–9*. Then discuss question 6 on the resource sheet.

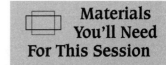

Materials You'll Need For This Session

Resource Sheet 2E

Accountability Partners

Have partners meet and discuss these questions together:

• How can I make God more real in my life throughout this coming week?

• How can we hold each other accountable to Bible reading and prayer so that we can both make God more real in our lives?

• How can I help make God more real in someone else's life? Who?

OPTION
Memory Verse

"The heavens declare the glory of God; the skies proclaim the work of his hands. Day after day they pour forth speech; night after night they display knowledge" (Psalm 19:1, 2).

TAKING THE NEXT STEP

Use questions 7–9 on the resource sheet to help participants apply this Bible study to their lives.

Close this session by saying, **Another text from the Bible gives a hint of God's extended thoughts: "But God demonstrates his own love for us in this: While we were still sinners, Christ died for us" (Romans 5:8). Men and women of the earth *do* matter to God. He is real and he cares about us. What significance that brings to our daily living! This is a foundational truth for all of life!**

CAN TRUTH EXIST APART FROM GOD?

Read the following passage from Faith's Fundamentals, *and list as many reasons as you can why truth can exist only if God is real.*

This is why the existence of God is fundamental. Man is finite, bound by an egocentric predicament, but God is not. God is infinite in every respect, including his knowledge. He is omniscient. He knows all things, and he knows them absolutely. His knowledge is complete and perfect. Absolute truth does exist: it is the contents of the mind of God.

The difference between God and man is rooted in the fact of creation. Man is in every respect a creature, and so is limited by nature. God alone is the Creator, the eternal one who brought man and everything else into existence out of nothing—*ex nihilo.* The distinction between Creator and creature is fundamental; it is the most important of all distinctions. The uncreated Creator is a unique kind of being. He transcends all the limitations by which creatures are inherently bound.

The existence of the transcendent Creator-God is the basis of absolutes of any kind. The mind of God is the prototype of all reason and logic. His very essence is *logos:* "word, reason, logic" (John 1:1). . . .

Here is an important point. This connection between God and truth exists *only* if God is truly the *ex nihilo* Creator of everything distinct from himself. . . . No other concept of God makes absolute truth possible. Without a Creator-God we are doomed to relativism.

▲   ▼   ▲

What Scripture Says
About
God and Truth

Read Romans 1:18–25 and consider the questions
that discuss God's relationship to the truth.

Verses 18–20

Who is suppressing the truth?

What truth do you think they are suppressing?

Why are they suppressing the truth?

How does God show himself to our inner moral sense?

How does God show himself through what he has created?

Verses 21–25

What did people who knew God do?

Why would people who know the true God make other gods?

What did God do to these people?

Why does Paul make a distinction between "created things" and "Creator"?

TEST YOUR KNOWLEDGE ON
World Religions

Below is a list of world religions. The column on the right describes at least one difference between the god of the world religions and the God of Jesus Christ. Match each religion by its unique belief about its god by drawing a line from each religion in the left column to the best description in the right.

Hinduism

God is one and his people are still waiting for the Messiah to come.

Islam

This popular movement inherited its roots from eastern religions.

Judaism

This eastern religion does not believe in the existence of a personal God.

Buddhism

Jesus is a created being, and the doctrine of the Trinity is from Satan.

New Age Movement

There is no God but Allah, and he is separate from the world.

Deism

God was once as we are now and, like him, we can become a god.

Jehovah's Witnesses

Brahman takes form in millions of lesser gods.

Mormonism

God created the world, but he does not intervene into its history.

Enlightening the "DARKENED HEART"

Review Romans 1:18–23 and answer the following questions.

1. In what ways is the truth about God and his existence suppressed in today's world?

2. What ways could you, your church, or your group be contributing to this suppression of God's truth?

3. What three things can you, your church, or your Bible study group do beginning this week to proclaim God and his truth?

Small Group Discussion

CONSIDERING SCRIPTURE

Romans 1:18–32

1. What can you know about God by simply observing the world around you?
   a. His incredible power
   b. His intricate designing ability
   c. His orderly systems organization
   d. His artistic creativity
   e. His understanding of meaningful relationships
   f. His high communication-systems design
   g. Other

2. What do you think is the best way to learn about God through nature?
   a. Observation (using the five senses—i.e., observing a sunset, the stars, the tides)
   b. Questioning (participation in problem-solving situations in nature—i.e., cycles and seasons and the effect on plants and animals)
   c. Violent impact (natural forces at work inciting fear or awe—i.e., storms, earthquakes, wind, weather, sun)
   d. Conversations with intelligent people (Questions of how, why, who, and where all lead to a creator.)

3. Why do you think some people worship and serve created things rather than the Creator?
   a. Selfishness—they see themselves as the center of their universe.
   b. Environment—they live in a godless void and have no information about God.
   c. Sin—they are aware of their own faults and do not want to be declared guilty.
   d. Human Example—Their teachers or mentors had already excepted a godless lifestyle.

4. What do you think is the main reason people turn to "every kind of wickedness, evil, greed and depravity"?
   a. They are not accountable to anyone except themselves.
   b. They have no foundation of truth to measure their actions against.
   c. Their minds, hearts, and spirits are not in line with God, and so they are under the control of the evil one.
   d. Their consciences no longer function to compare what they do with what they know is right or wrong.

5. Do you agree or disagree that God has somehow built into every human being an "inner sense" of what God requires? Explain your comment.

Psalm 19:1–6; Psalm 8:3–9

6. What in God's creation proclaims his reality most clearly?
   a. The heavens themselves demand some explanation. A big bang and undirected evolution does not make sense when one views the stars.
   b. The meaningful order of the created world has made this planet an Eden in many places. It is noticed by young and old alike
   c. The heavens say this universe is more complicated than we ever imagined. It has a designer and architect. Beware and give honor where it is due!
   d. Human beings are the crowning glory to this unique planet's created jewels. Their bodies' intricate design, along with their rational minds, speak loudly about a thoughtful designer.

TAKING THE NEXT STEP

7. Like David, most of us have at some time gazed at the heavens and wondered how the Creator of the universe could be mindful and care about our lives. How does the vastness of the universe and the greatness of the Creator make you feel about your life?
   a. Filled with a sense of awe of God and his majesty
   b. Overwhelmed that he would hear, pay attention to, and answer my prayers
   c. Privileged that I have received incredible blessings by his strong hand
   d. Grateful for my eyes so that I can see the wonder of the Lord
   e. I've never given much thought to how God is mindful of my life
   f. I don't gaze at the heavens

8. How important do you feel you are to God? (Place a dot on the scale.)

VERY IMPORTANT   NOT AT ALL IMPORTANT

9. What difference does it make in your day-to-day life to know that God cares about you as an individual? (Place a dot on the scale.)

BIG DIFFERENCE   NO DIFFERENCE

Fundamental #3

The Bible Is God's Word

*I*n one sense any building's foundation is its most important part. It supports everything else related to the building. Thus we feel happy and secure when our house or school or church is resting on a good foundation.

Jesus talks about the proper foundation for our lives in his familiar parable of the wise and foolish builders (Matthew 7:24–27). He says that his spoken words are like a foundation of solid rock. A life built upon his words will not fall.

Ephesians 2:20 says that the church itself is "built upon the foundation of the apostles and prophets." In what sense can the church be built upon apostles and prophets? Ephesians 3:5 shows us the answer: *God's Word,* revealed to them through the Spirit, forms a foundation for the church.

The fundamental importance of the words of Christ, and the words of God in general, leads us to ask these questions: Where do we find these words today? Do we have any sure access to these holy and life-giving words?

The answer is *yes*—the very words of God are present to us today in the form of the Bible.

—Jack Cottrell, *Faith's Fundamentals*

Central Theme	The Bible is God's Word and is thus the foundation for truth.
Lesson Aim	Students will understand four things about the Bible: • What the Bible is (the Word of God) • How the Bible came about • How to interpret God's Word • How to build a lasting foundation on God's Word
Bible Background	Matthew 7:15–27
For Further Study	Read Chapter Three of *Faith's Fundamentals*.

PLAN ONE

Classes

BUILDING COMMUNITY

Ask the class, **What is your all-time favorite literary work, and why?** Give each person an opportunity to answer this question. Let the class know it has to be a book other than the Bible. After each one has had an opportunity to respond, ask the class to reflect silently or aloud on the following question: **Would you stake your future on the contents of your favorite literary work?**

Each of us has a book we call our favorite. But to base our future and eternity on that book is another matter. The Bible is for many a favorite literary work. To some, that is all the Bible is. But others stake their future, their very lives on it. What is so important about the Bible that makes it different from all other books?

To answer this question, we must first consider how the Bible originated. There are two basic theories. One theory says the Bible has a divine origin; the other says the Bible originated with man. This latter view teaches that the Bible is not a unique book. Rather, it is merely a collection of writings about one religious faith that is no more or less accurate than another religious faith. In reference to this line of thought, Jack Cottrell writes in *Faith's Fundamentals,*

In eighteenth-century Europe a number of writers had already begun to attack the divine origin of Scripture in the name of higher biblical criticism. Nineteenth-century critics focused on the first five books of the Bible, traditionally held to be written by Moses by the inspiration of the Holy Spirit. The critics divided these "five books of Moses" among at least four anonymous writers and editors, labeled simply *J, E, D,* and *P.*

These critics believed the Bible came about through human invention. As a part of this human invention, the Bible is believed to have gone through an evolutionary process. In the early stages of Jewish history, say these critics, the Jews had a primitive concept of God. As time went by, the Jews began to refine their view of God. This process continued through Jesus' day so that even what Jesus said cannot be considered

Literary Launch
10 Minutes

Mini-lecture
5 Minutes

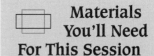

Materials You'll Need For This Session

Resource Sheets 3A–3C, Transparency 3A, erasable marker

absolute. Therefore, relativism prevails, and what may be true today about God may not be true tomorrow.

This system of higher criticism continues to be a force in the world in which we live. This is one reason why many have a difficult time believing that the Bible is unique in comparison to all other books. What does the Bible have to say about its origin? To begin to investigate this, we must first understand how God communicates to his people.

CONSIDERING SCRIPTURE

How God Communicates
15 Minutes

Hand out copies of Resource Sheet 3A and ask the class to form groups of five to seven people each. In their groups, have them read the instructions at the top of the resource sheet and then answer the questions that follow. After about ten minutes, ask the class to come back together again, and take five minutes to review their answers. The focus of this exercise is to help students learn that **God communicates to us through the Bible and we can trust it to give us the message of salvation. However, just to say the Bible is God's Word may not take away any doubt we may have about it being from God. When we are confronted with God's Word, we must make a choice, either to accept it or to reject it. The only way we can believe in God's Word is by faith.**

The Importance of God's Word
10 Minutes

With the class together in one large group, hand out Resource Sheet 3B. Use the top portion of the sheet for this activity. Ask for a volunteer to read *Matthew 7:24–27,* and then lead the class in discovering the similarities and differences between the two builders. The point of this exercise is to show that God's Word is the truth and the truth is always the foundation on which to build our lives.

Properly Understanding God's Word
10 Minutes

If the Bible is to be our foundation, all people should be able to clearly understand the Bible. Then, why are there so many different interpretations? Jack Cottrell suggests there are three principles by which we can have certainty about our own particular interpretations and convictions of what God says to us through his Word.

Display Transparency 3A. Reveal one principle at a time. With a transparency marker, highlight key words for emphasis in each of the principles as the class discusses them.

Read *Acts 8:26–39* and discuss how these three principles are evident in this passage.

Here are some additional helps from *Faith's Fundamentals* pertaining to each principle:

1. Study the Bible holistically.

"A basic rule of interpretation is that the less clear must be seen in the light of the more clear. . . .

"The eunuch did not understand the text because he did not yet have the whole picture of God's revelation. He did not know Jesus Christ and the New Covenant. On the other hand, Philip did have this whole picture.

"Likewise, today we can be more sure of our understanding of the Bible when we have studied it holistically, either on our own or at the feet of a teacher who has already done so."

2. Interpret personal experiences by the Bible, not the Bible by personal experiences.

"Like Philip and the eunuch, we must begin with Scripture (Acts 8:35) and let our experiences conform to what it says. We fall into grievous error when we base our conclusions about biblical truth on personal experience."

3. Be willing to accept the truth even when it means changing your lifestyle.

"The real barrier to true biblical understanding is not a sin-clouded intellect but a sin-hardened will. The problem is not inability to see the truth, but unwillingness to accept the truth."

TAKING THE NEXT STEP

Use the bottom portion of Resource Sheet 3B for this activity. Have students pair up with partners to discuss the questions for about five to seven minutes. Then ask them to pray about the priorities they have set.

Building on a Firm Foundation
10 Minutes

PLAN TWO  **Groups**

BUILDING COMMUNITY

• How would you answer a skeptic who asked you to prove that the Bible is true or that it is the Word of God?

• OPTION: When did the Bible become more than just an old book full of stories, fables, or myths to you?

CONSIDERING SCRIPTURE

Distribute copies of <u>Resource Sheet 3C</u>. As they are being passed around, say, **The Bible was written by many different men through the inspiration of the Holy Spirit over a long period of time. It contains words of history, poetry, and prophesy. It presents essays on life, succinct phrases of wisdom and truth, lyrics of songs, biographies, letters of encouragement, instruction in theology, and visions of the end of the world and future life in Heaven. In one section, it contains quotations of Jesus of Nazareth, the "Son of God" on earth in the flesh of man. He explained some of the "truth" of God's Word, which we'll study in this lesson.**

Jesus emphasized two issues in these verses. The first is that not all teachers of "truth" come from God, and so people must beware. They should recognize and pay close attention to the truth of God's Word. Second, as a foundation to life it is critical to apply God's Word to the practice of daily living for life to not come crashing down.

Listen closely to the following teaching of Jesus. He emphasizes strongly that it matters whether or not we pay attention to the words of God.

Read *Matthew 7:15–27*. Then discuss questions 1–4 on the resource sheet.

After discussing question 4, ask someone to read *2 Timothy 3:16, 17*. Then discuss questions 5 and 6 on the resource sheet. Before the volunteer reads the Scripture, make these comments: **In the following Scripture passage, the Bible says two things about itself. First, all of it is from God. Second, it has been given to us so that our lives may be improved. The Bible is not just a collection of stories, fables, or myths; it is a "revelation" of**

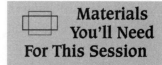

Materials You'll Need For This Session

Resource Sheet 3C

OPTION
Accountability Partners

Ask accountability partners to discuss question 8 on Resource Sheet 3C. Encourage them to talk about how well they are doing in their daily Bible-reading times. They can also discuss what they learned from this past week's Bible studies.

OPTION
Memory Verse

"For prophecy never had its origin in the will of man, but men spoke from God as they were carried along by the Holy Spirit" (2 Peter 1:21).

God's truth to the world. It is not a book of human thought or philosophy; it is a reflection of God's essence and innermost heart.

After discussing question 6, summarize with these thoughts: **Finally, the Bible explains how the God-breathed Word was recorded for us. The process was called "inspiration." Each writer penned the words from his own cultural and historical background and his own personal experience. Even though the writers used their own thinking, education, language, and style, their writing was the reflection of what God wanted people to know. Because of this, the Bible can be trusted because God controlled its authorship. Its words are authoritative for our faith and daily living. Second Peter 1:21 says, "For prophecy never had its origin in the will of man, but men spoke from God as they were carried along by the Holy Spirit."**

TAKING THE NEXT STEP

Now that we have studied what the Bible says about itself, how would you begin to answer someone who asked you to prove the Bible is God's Word?

After discussing the preceding question, discuss questions 7 and 8 on the resource sheet.

Close the session by saying, **In *Faith's Fundamentals,* Jack Cottrell says this about the importance of God's Word:**

We cannot be sure that we are understanding the Bible correctly until in our hearts we have put everything on the line, until we are willing to risk everything—pride, family, friends, job, pension—in our quest for true understanding of God's Word. The Holy Spirit's proper role in this process is to give us the moral power to subordinate our wills to the clear Word of God.

May you desire with all your heart to know and obey the Word of God for the rest of your lives here on the earth!

HOW DOES GOD

TO US?

Read each question and then look up the corresponding Bible verses to help you respond.

1. In what ways has God communicated his Word to his people?
Exodus 6:28—7:6; Matthew 3:13–17; Luke 1:26–29; Hebrews 1:1, 2

2. Where do we have access to these words today?
Ephesians 3:2–6; 2 Peter 1:19–21 (cf. Hebrews 1:1, 2)

3. Can we be certain that God's agents got the message right and that they did not forget something important? Why or why not?
Romans 15:4; 2 Timothy 3:14–17

4. What does it take on our part to accept the Bible as God's Word?
John 20:30, 31; Romans 10:16–18

DISCOVERING THE IMPORTANCE OF GOD'S WORD IN OUR LIVES

Read Matthew 7:24–27 and complete the list below by identifying
the differences and similarities between the two builders Jesus talked about.

DIFFERENCES:

SIMILARITIES:

What point was Jesus making in this parable?

BUILDING ON A FIRM FOUNDATION

*"Am I truly basing my beliefs, my values, and my life on the
teachings of God's Word? If not Scripture, what?"*
—*Jack Cottrell,* Faith's Fundamentals

How would you respond to this question?
**In order to build my beliefs, values, and life on a firm foundation I need to
(list in order of priority):**

①

②

③

④

⑤

⑥

⑦

Small Group Discussion

CONSIDERING SCRIPTURE
Matthew 7:15–27

1. What is the best way to know when teachers are telling the truth?
   a. Their actions when not in front of a crowd correspond to what they say.
   b. Their personal financial investments authenticate their teachings.
   c. Their personal stories of struggle and sacrifice transparently model their teaching.
   d. Their personal decisions for the future reflect a commitment to the principles they espouse.

2. What do you think would be the best "good fruit" in the life of a teacher of God's truth?
   a. Oranges—a great source of Vitamin C—reflecting an energized life from regular input from the Word of God through the power of the Holy Spirit.
   b. Apples—representing consistent good health. An apple a day keeps the doctor away, especially as received from a daily quiet time with the Lord.
   c. Plums—thick and juicy throughout their branches—a fruit abundantly provided, generously shared, and tasty to all who eat. Their personal character reflects a source of health, integrity, and generosity for all.
   d. Peaches—sweet. The words from their mouths are luscious and refreshing to all who hear.

3. Why do you think prophesying, driving out demons, and performing miracles are not an accurate indication of a "truth teller"?
   a. Outward spiritual signs could be just a show, covering up an unauthentic life.
   b. These signs will draw crowds, but they will not necessarily assist leaders to help the church move to a deeper spiritual ministry.
   c. They might be a sidetrack that makes the teacher feel important, but in reality he is very shallow in his spiritual walk.
   d. These spiritual signs do not require the preaching or teaching of the Word. The performer could have a shallow spiritual life and still be successful.

4. Why do you think Jesus placed such emphasis on the application of God's Word to life?
   a. The applied Word changes a life.
   b. It's easy to be a hearer and not a doer.
   c. It's not until the truth is applied in a life that it is really learned.
   d. Sometimes it is hard to be even a good listener to the Word. This emphasis helps all those who have trouble listening and concentrating.

2 Timothy 3:16, 17

5. Why is Scripture trustworthy only if God was in control of its writing?
   a. People are too opinionated and would go their own directions.
   b. Only God knows the heart of people. He knows what would help believers become world Christians.
   c. God does all the connecting that happens in a ministry and makes it work in the life of the church.
   d. God is the only one with the whole perspective and future vision.

6. If the Bible was written under God's control, what authority does it have in people's lives?
   a. No authority. People need to make up their own minds about what is right and wrong.
   b. Some authority. People need to listen to God's Word, but sometimes we have to do what we think is right in a situation.
   c. Full authority. God's Word says it, I believe it, that settles it.
   d. What authority? It has influence only if one reads it.

TAKING THE NEXT STEP

7. Since the Word of God was given to us not just to win arguments but to change our lives and help us know how to do the work of God in the world, how do you think God wants us to respond to his revelation?
   a. To consume it as the mainstay of our spiritual diet
   b. To actively find a place in our schedule to implement the new truth instantly
   c. Before we know everything, to do everything we know
   d. To be open to new thoughts—God has new ideas for us when we are willing to try something new
   e. To start reading the Bible more regularly

8. What will it take for you to begin reading God's Word regularly, discover his truth, and become confident in your faith?
   a. Changing my priorities
   b. Changing my schedule
   c. Changing my mind
   d. Changing my attitudes
   e. A little help from my friends

Principles of BIBLE INTERPRETATION
from *Faith's Fundamentals*

1. **Study the Bible holistically.**

2. **Interpret personal experiences by the Bible, not the Bible by personal experiences.**

3. **Be willing to accept the truth even when it means changing your lifestyle.**

Fundamental #4

Jesus Is Our Savior

When Peter said of Jesus, "Thou art the Christ," he was identifying him as the long-awaited, divinely sent Savior. Although at that point he did not yet understand *how* Jesus would work his work of salvation (see Matthew 16:21–23), Peter knew that Jesus was indeed the one anointed by God to save the world.

Likewise, when we confess "Jesus is the Christ," we are acknowledging him as our only Savior and are declaring that this will be our relationship to him from this point forward. We are affirming the truth of Paul's statement, "that Christ Jesus came into the world to save sinners" (1 Timothy 1:15).

It is not enough to relate to Jesus just as the incarnation and model of true godhood among us. Nor is it enough to look to him simply as the model of a perfect human life. He cannot be to us just a teacher of proper values, or an inspiring leader, or a friend to quell our loneliness. He is indeed all of these things, but none of them is the essential aspect of his messiahship. What is essential and most important is that he is our *Savior*. This is how we must think of him and relate to him first of all.

—Jack Cottrell, *Faith's Fundamentals*

Central Theme   Jesus is the only way to salvation.

Lesson Aim   The student will:
- Be able to explain the meaning of the term *Christ*
- Be able to explain why Jesus is the Christ
- Be able to share Jesus as Savior with a friend

Bible Background   Matthew 16:13–17

For Further Study   Read Chapter Four of *Faith's Fundamentals*.

PLAN ONE

Classes

BUILDING COMMUNITY

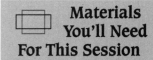

Display <u>Transparency 4A</u> or write the questions from the transparency master on the chalkboard. Only show the top half of the transparency sheet displaying the following question: **"Who was your hero when you were growing up and why?"** If your class has fewer than fifteen people, take time to get a response from everyone. After the class has responded, reveal the follow-up question at the bottom of the transparency.

Say, **When we were young, we all had someone we called a hero, whether fictitious or real. What are the qualities of a hero?** Underneath this question on the transparency, list the qualities that the class mentions. This list may include: physical strength, ability to fly, always conquers villains, always does good, kindness, an advocate for the weak, bravery, always there when you need him or her.

Do you think Jesus has the stuff heroes are made of? Some people say that Jesus was merely a good man or a wise teacher. Some people call him a hero. If we believe Jesus is the only way to God, then he must have qualities that set him above all other heroes. The task before us in this session is to determine what is so unique about Jesus that sets him apart from all other men and heroes.

Ask a volunteer to read aloud *Matthew 16:13–17*. Then say, **When we become a Christian we confess that Jesus is the Christ, just as Peter confessed Jesus to be the Christ. Do we really know what we mean when we call Jesus the "Christ"? Is the word *Christ* simply Jesus' last name, or does it mean something more?**

Ask the class to work in groups of five to seven people each. Give the groups a word-study assignment investigating the word *Christ*. Provide each group with a blank sheet of paper, English and Bible dictionaries, commentaries that cover Matthew 16:13–17, and, if available, word-study books. Or make one or two of each available for all the groups to share. (If you do not own some of these resources, check your church library or ask a leader in the church.) Have the groups use these tools to write a one- or two-paragraph description on what it means for Jesus to be the "Christ." After about ten minutes, allow time for each group to share that description with the rest of the class.

Super Hero
10 Minutes

> ### Materials You'll Need For This Session
>
> Paper, pens or pencils, overhead projector, English and Bible dictionaries, commentaries on Matthew, word study books, Resource Sheets 4A–4C, and Transparency 4A

Word Study
15 Minutes

Here are some quotes from *Faith's Fundamentals* you can use to aid the class in answering questions or by giving direction.

"Our English word *Christ* comes directly from the Greek term *christos,* which is a translation of the Hebrew term *mashiach* (from which we get our English word *Messiah).* Both the Greek and Hebrew words mean 'the anointed one.' So when we confess Jesus is the Christ, we are confessing him to be the anointed one."

"Literally [anointing] was the pouring of oil (such as olive oil) on a person's head. In the history of Israel this was like an ordination service that conferred God's blessing on a person chosen to fill an office of leadership."

"When Peter said of Jesus, 'Thou art the Christ,' he was identifying him as the long-awaited, divinely sent Savior."

"When we confess 'Jesus is the Christ,' we are acknowledging him as our only Savior and are declaring that this will be our relationship to him from this point forward."

"[Jesus] cannot be to us just a teacher of proper values, or an inspiring leader, or a friend to quell our loneliness. He is indeed all of these things, but none of them is the essential aspect of his messiahship. What is essential and most important is that he is our *Savior.* This is how we must think of him and relate to him first of all."

CONSIDERING SCRIPTURE

Study the Scriptures
15 Minutes

After Peter confessed Jesus to be the Christ, Jesus told his disciples he was going to die and then rise from the dead on the third day. Jack Cottrell writes, "Christ's death and resurrection are the two primary pillars of his saving work They are the chief elements of the gospel." While we believe Jesus is the Christ, the question then is, "What do his death and resurrection mean in regard to our salvation in Jesus Christ?"

Hand out Resource Sheet 4A and have the class work in groups of five to seven each. Challenge the class to determine the significance of Christ's death and resurrection and then to explain why God had to go through such extreme measures to save us. Tell them they have fifteen minutes to complete this activity.

Many of the responses below are suggested in chapter four of *Faith's Fundamentals.* Use these suggestions if needed as a guide to help the groups through their discussion. If time allows, ask if there are any questions that were raised as the groups studied the passages listed on Resource Sheet 4A.

What was the significance of Jesus' death?

Romans 5:10—It reconciles us to God.

Galatians 3:13—He took the curse in our place.

Hebrews 2:14, 15—It renders Satan powerless.

Hebrews 9:28—He took our sins upon himself.

1 Peter 2:24—He healed us from our sins.

What was the significance of Jesus' resurrection?

Acts 2:32–36—It demonstrates Jesus' lordship.

1 John 3:8—It destroys the work of Jesus' enemies.

Daniel 2:44—It inaugurates Jesus' kingdom.

Colossians 2:12—It validates the cross.

1 Corinthians 15:20–22—It invigorates the dead.

Why should our salvation require such extreme measures?

Romans 3:26—So God can be just and can be the justifier.

Hebrews 12:22–29—To satisfy God's wrath.

1 John 4:8–10—Because God is love and wants to save us.

TAKING THE NEXT STEP

Have class members pair up with one another, and then hand them copies of Resource Sheet 4B. Challenge them to consider what impact Jesus has made on their lives. Have them use the outline provided on the resource sheet. Tell the class they have ten minutes to write their testimonies, and then they will have three minutes each to share their testimonies with their partners. After the testimonies have been shared, say, **With whom could you share your testimony? Do you have a friend, co-worker, family member, or neighbor who doesn't know Christ? Talk briefly about this person with your partner.**

Close the session with prayer covering these three thoughts: (1) Ask God to open the heart of a friend. (2) Ask God to open the door of opportunity to share Christ with that friend. (3) Ask God to open our mouths to share Christ with our friends.

Testimony Sharing
20 Minutes

PLAN TWO  roups

BUILDING COMMUNITY

As participants are getting settled, give each one a copy of Resource Sheet 4C. Start the meeting with question 1.

CONSIDERING SCRIPTURE

We live in an age when "saviors"—that is, people who heroically come to the aid of and save others—are appreciated whenever they appear, but they are rare and are rarely expected. When we look to people to fill that role, they usually don't live up to our expectations. That leaves us in a quandary with only the bad situation and our own ingenuity to handle the problem. It is unfortunately not uncommon to be in a situation where there is no hope and no way out. This lesson explores the role Jesus plays as a savior for the world.

Ask two volunteers to read *Matthew 1:20, 21* and *Luke 2:10, 11* aloud. Then discuss questions 2–5 on the resource sheet.

After discussing question 5, make a transition into the next part of the Bible study by saying, **The angel's announcement that explained this unique birth was given because the babe would ultimately save his people from their sins. His name, *Jesus,* meant "the Lord saves." Upon Jesus' birth into the world, his baby announcement by an angelic host was that "a Savior" had finally arrived. The Greek word for the angel's "good news" is more often translated as the word *gospel.* The essence of the gospel is that Christ was born to be "the Savior for all people." He didn't come to help people save themselves, he came to *be* their Savior.**

Now ask a volunteer to read *Matthew 16:13–17.* Before the passage is read, say, **Notice that as an adult and now a sought-after rabbi, Jesus accepted the designation "Christ." This was the Greek word for the Aramaic word, *Messiah.*** After the Scripture passage is read, discuss questions 6 and 7 on the resource sheet.

Continue the Bible study by having volunteers read the Scripture passage for each of the following sections on the resource sheet, and then discuss the corresponding questions.

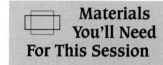

Materials You'll Need For This Session

Resource Sheet 4C

Accountability Partners

• If everyone in your group is already a Christian, ask partners to talk about when they first accepted Jesus as Savior. Challenge them to discuss how Christ's salvation influences their day-to-day lives.

• If some participants are not Christians, you can suggest that the partners meet during the week, at which time the Christian partners could share testimonies or explain the gospel more fully. The Christians could use the simple testimony outline on Resource Sheet 4B or other printed materials to help them explain the gospel message clearly.

OPTION
Memory Verse

"God . . . has saved us and called us to a holy life—not because of anything we have done but because of his own purpose and grace. This grace was given us in Christ Jesus before the beginning of time, but it has now been revealed through the appearing of our Savior, Christ Jesus, who has destroyed death" (2 Timothy 1:8–10).

TAKING THE NEXT STEP

Jack Cottrell states in *Faith's Fundamentals,*

> **Here is the point that must not be missed. When Christ "bore our sins" and became a curse for us, he took upon himself the *whole* penalty for *all* the sins of the *whole* human race. This means not only that he was suffering physical death in his body, but also that he was suffering in his heart and soul the equivalent of eternal death in hell for every member of the human race.**

Close this session by discussing question 12 on the resource sheet.

TWO PILLARS
of Christ's Saving Work

There are two primary pillars of Jesus' saving work. These two pillars are Jesus' death on the cross and his bodily resurrection from the dead. But what is the significance of these two saving works of Christ? Look up the following Scriptures and list by each reference the significance of Jesus' death and resurrection in regard to our salvation.

What was the significance of Jesus' death?

• Romans 5:10—

• Galatians 3:13—

• Hebrews 2:14, 15—

• Hebrews 9:28—

• 1 Peter 2:24—

What was the significance of Jesus' resurrection?

• Acts 2:32–36—

• 1 John 3:8—

• Daniel 2:44—

• Colossians 2:12—

• 1 Corinthians 15:20–22—

Why should our salvation require such extreme measures?

• Romans 3:26—

• Hebrews 12:22–29—

• 1 John 4:8–10—

My Testimony

Jesus Christ is the only Savior of the world. The only way the world will know Jesus is if people have an opportunity to hear about him. Providing those who need Jesus with an opportunity to hear means that we must be able to share a verbal testimony about Jesus. Use the headings below as your outline. Use only the space that is provided on this side of the paper. People will be more likely to listen to a testimony that is to the point than one that goes on and on.

MY LIFE BEFORE I FOUND JESUS:

HOW I FOUND JESUS:

MY LIFE AFTER I FOUND JESUS:

Small Group Discussion

BUILDING COMMUNITY

1. Have you ever found yourself in the middle of a hard situation when a "savior" came to the rescue and snatched you from the brink of disaster? Briefly tell the group the story, using these details.
   - What was the situation?
   - How did you feel in the midst of the situation?
   - How were you "saved"?
   - How did you feel after the situation was over?

CONSIDERING SCRIPTURE

Matthew 1:20, 21; Luke 2:10, 11

2. What do you think was the significance of the angel's instruction to Joseph about the special name to be given to the child?
   a. This child will reflect a special touch of God, so watch out.
   b. This child will have a bigger future than you can imagine, so don't try to explain his conception.
   c. This child has been given an assigned mission in life, so get ready.
   d. This child is the one you have been waiting for.

3. What do you think was the shepherds' situation that made the angelic announcement of a "savior" good news to them?
   a. They had previously seen no hope for the future with a cruel king like Herod.
   b. They felt stuck in their jobs.
   c. They saw themselves in a hopeless situation.
   d. Their only hope was that someday a military leader would arise and oust the Roman rule.

4. How do you think they felt about the arrival of a Savior?
   a. Hope had come.
   b. Bondage had its end in sight.
   c. Freedom and peace might be seen in their lifetime.
   d. God must have heard their prayers!
   e. I have no idea.

5. How do you feel about the arrival of a Savior on earth?
   a. Just what we needed!
   b. The angelic introduction was the event of the millennium.
   c. God really cares about people on earth!
   d. Could it be that Jesus was born to save me from my sins?

Matthew 16:13–17

6. What do you think are the most important similarities between a "messiah" and a "savior"?
   a. They both bring hope to an otherwise hopeless situation.
   b. They are leaders to those who are unable to move forward.
   c. They remove a person from a dangerous situation to safety.
   d. Their possible existence motivates one to hang on a little longer in a hard situation.

7. How do you feel about Jesus' response to Peter's answer?
   a. Jesus knew that Peter needed help putting his thoughts into words.
   b. Thumbs up! Jesus affirmed Peter and his expression of faith.
   c. This "blessing" by Jesus could very well have been the foundation of spiritual strength that held up the rest of Peter's ministry.
   d. In some small way I can identify with the feelings of Jesus every time I witness someone declare faith in Jesus in a public setting.

Acts 5:30–32

8. What do you think is the most important part of the salvation that has been given to men?
   a. Forgiveness of all sin
   b. Peace with God after a lifetime of war with him
   c. Power by the indwelling Holy Spirit to overcome the evil one and his control
   d. The "gift" from God that helps us through this life and then guarantees our eternal life after death with God

Titus 2:11–14

9. What do you think is the greatest practical impact on our lives from receiving the gift of salvation?
   a. We can learn how to say no to worldly passions and unholy living.
   b. We can become people of integrity with lives that reflect truth and honesty.
   c. We can become inwardly stronger and more mature, reflecting a greater personal character with obvious caring and a desire to do what is good.
   d. We can have an inner strength to wait upon God for his perfect timing in the things of life and ultimately the return of Jesus.

continued on next page

10. How do you feel about having been redeemed and made pure in God's sight?
   a. Overwhelmed. How could God do this?
   b. Embarrassed. So much more of my past life shows than I previously thought really mattered.
   c. Clean and new. I'm ready to move forward.
   d. Grateful. God has done wonderful things in my life.

2 Timothy 1:8–12

11. Which aspect of destroying death and bringing life and immortality to light has the greatest impact on our lives?
   a. The removal of the fear of separation from loved ones and God because of the wrongs in our lives
   b. The opening of our eyes to see past present troubles
   c. Hearing the call of God to respond to the future with a completely new purpose for existence
   d. Trusting in the security of his promises that whatever happens in the future, we are not alone

TAKING THE NEXT STEP

12. What will you do with the salvation that has been given to you in light of the cost required to provide it?
   a. Mull it over and try to sort out what it means for me
   b. Act right now and receive Christ as my Savior and supreme authority
   c. Reestablish my life as one that belongs to the Lord of life, Jesus Christ
   d. Rest in this truth with a heart full of gratitude, and stay available to do good works as led by the Lord on a daily basis

Who was your hero when you were growing up and why?

✦ ✦ ✦

What are the qualities of a hero?

Jesus Is God's Son

*J*esus' first disciples and the first Christians had one thing in common: they were all Jews. Thus their understanding of the identity of Jesus was based largely on the Old Testament and its prophecies of the coming Messiah.

These prophecies include two distinct strands. First, it was foretold that "a Redeemer will come to Zion" to save his people (Isaiah 59:20). The Redeemer describes his work like this: "The Lord has anointed me to bring good news to the afflicted; He has sent me to bind up the brokenhearted, to proclaim liberty to captives, and freedom to prisoners; to proclaim the favorable year of the Lord" (Isaiah 61:1, 2; see Luke 4:17–21).

Second, the Old Testament foretold that God himself would personally come to save his people. "'Comfort, O comfort My people,' says your God. . . . A voice is calling, 'Clear the way for the Lord in the wilderness; make smooth in the desert a highway for our God'" (Isaiah 40:1, 3). "'Behold, I am going to send My messenger, and he will clear the way before Me. And the Lord, whom you seek, will suddenly come to His temple . . . ,' says the Lord of hosts" (Malachi 3:1).

These two strands of prophecy were brought together in Jesus of Nazareth. Not only was he the Christ, the one anointed to save, he was also the Son of God, the divine Lord himself.

—Jack Cottrell, *Faith's Fundamentals*

Central Theme	Jesus was more than a man, he is God.
Lesson Aim	Students will: • Be able to explain why Jesus is God • Reflect how Jesus has changed lives and consider areas in their lives that need to change
Bible Background	Colossians 1:15–23
For Further Study	Read Chapter Five of *Faith's Fundamentals*.

Classes

BUILDING COMMUNITY

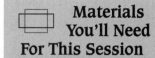 Display <u>Transparency 5A</u>. Introduce the question on the sheet by saying, **Two TV shows of the 1960s portrayed two women who, through the wonder of television, were able to perform supernatural feats. The leading characters of the two shows were Samantha of "Bewitched" and Jeannie of "I Dream of Jeannie." To this day a vital question in TV trivia is, "Who was more powerful: Samantha or Jeannie?"** Use the section provided on Transparency 5A to keep track of the votes.

Once voting is completed, say, **This question does not condone witchcraft or any power separate from God. Rather, it was asked to help us consider the person of Jesus. With today's prevailing relativism, Jesus is viewed on the same plane as founders of other religions, such as Muhammad or Buddha. In other words, Jesus was merely a great teacher or prophet. What would you say to a friend who couldn't say for certain who was more powerful, Jesus or Muhammad? To understand who Jesus is, we must go to the Bible.**

Who's More Powerful?
10 Minutes

Materials You'll Need For This Session

Resource Sheets 5A–5C, Transparency 5A, erasable transparency pens, English and Bible dictionaries

---

CONSIDERING SCRIPTURE

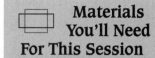 Hand out copies of <u>Resource Sheet 5A</u>. Ask the class to divide into groups of five to seven each. The goal of this exercise is to help students discover through Scripture that Jesus really is God, not just a good man or a wise teacher. Below are the answers to Resource Sheet 5A.

Check the References
15 Minutes

	DESCRIBES JESUS	DESCRIBES THE FATHER
Invisible		✓
Firstborn	✓	
Created All Things	✓	✓
All Things Created for Himself	✓	✓
Existed Before Anything Else Was Created	✓	✓
Holds All of Creation Together	✓	✓
Head of the Church	✓	
Supreme Over All Things	✓	✓
Fully Divine	✓	✓
Reconciles Man to Himself	✓	✓

Give the class ten minutes to do this exercise. Keeping the class in their groups, take five minutes to review Resource Sheet 5A, focusing on the questions at the bottom of the sheet. The conclusion should be that Jesus is God. Even with the characteristics they do not share, there is very much a connection. The first example is that Jesus is the physical image of the invisible God. Second, God made Jesus to be the head of the church. There can be no doubt of the uniqueness and divinity of Christ.

Before and After
15 Minutes

Hand out copies of Resource Sheet 5B. This sheet continues the Bible study on Colossians 1:15–23. Ask the class to work in the same small groups to complete this exercise. The goal of this exercise is to teach students that it makes a difference in their lives that Jesus is God. If Jesus were not God, our faith would be in vain.

After the class has taken ten minutes to work on Resource Sheet 5B, take five minutes to find out how each group answered the "Digging Deeper" questions. Have English and Bible dictionaries available for the groups to use in answering these questions.

TAKING THE NEXT STEP

Under Construction
20 Minutes

Pass around copies of Resource Sheet 5C. For this section, the class can stay in their groups or come back together in one large group. Read the first two paragraphs of the resource sheet. Challenge students to take a few moments to consider at least three areas where they have seen Jesus' power and supremacy in their lives. After the class has taken time to write down three things, ask students to share with the class some of their responses.

Ask students to take a few moments to consider what changes they need to make in their lives because of who Jesus is. Challenge them with this question: **What areas in your life have you not submitted to Jesus Christ's authority? Four broad categories of our lives are listed at the bottom of the resource sheet: home life, marketplace, church, and recreation time.**

Tell the class, **You do not need to stick to these four areas alone. If you think of another area that needs Christ's work in your life, you can create that new category and write down the corresponding need.**

After the class has been given time to determine what changes need to take place in their lives, close the class time with prayer. Guide them first in silent prayer by speaking aloud the areas of our lives mentioned above: home life, marketplace, church, and recreation time. After mentioning each area, give members time to pray silently. Close the class time with your own final prayer thoughts.

PLAN TWO  **Groups**

BUILDING COMMUNITY

When was the very first time you remember hearing about Jesus?
- Tell your story.
- How old were you and what was the situation?
- You may change names to protect the "innocent" if necessary.

CONSIDERING SCRIPTURE

Jesus of Nazareth is not like any other person ever born. His origin was unique, having been born of a virgin mother. As his life unfolded, it became clear that he was a man living a life on purpose. His purpose was not to be a teacher, although he may have been the best that ever lived. He was not here to be a miracle worker, though no one has ever performed so many miracles of such a broad range as he did. His purpose on earth was as the "Son of God," to die as a substitutionary sacrifice in the place of all people. He came to provide a link between the fallen races of the earth and a holy God who longed for interaction and reunion with his creation. His death in the place of all people fulfilled the punishment required that was a result of their sin and fatal separation from God. His role as the God-man has never happened before or since, and it has given peace and hope to all who have put their faith and trust in his atoning work. In this lesson, we will see that Jesus really is the Son of God and why that is so important to our lives.

Distribute copies of Resource Sheet 5D. Ask two volunteers to read aloud this session's Scripture passages: *John 10:22–33* and *1 John 5:1–20.* After the first passage is read, the leader should begin by responding to question 1. Then the rest of the group may discuss other issues of the question until the discussion is complete. Then, go around the group and let each member take a turn being the first person to share his or her answer. After the first three questions have been discussed, have a volunteer read the second passage, and then continue discussing questions 4–7 in the same manner.

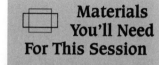

Materials You'll Need For This Session

Resource Sheet 5D

Accountability Partners

After answering the last question on the resource sheet, ask partners to get together and discuss their responses to question 9 in more detail. Also, encourage them to share with one another where they still need help in remembering that Jesus, as God's Son, is our source of power in daily struggles. Then they should pray for each other.

Memory Verse

"Who is it that overcomes the world? Only he who believes that Jesus is the Son of God" (1 John 5:5).

TAKING THE NEXT STEP

Jack Cottrell makes the following statement in *Faith's Fundamentals:*

> **The infinite power that flows from the risen Christ is able to redeem the universe itself, including our own mortal bodies (Romans 8:18-23). This is not merely a restoration of the old, original order of things, but an advance to a new and eternal and glorified state. Such an act of redemption is a combination of resurrection and creation—the two masterworks in the repertoire of divine omnipotence (Romans 4:17). It is the work of deity, the work of God's Son, Jesus.**

Conclude the session by reading *John 20:31* and then discussing the final two questions on the resource sheet.

Who Is Jesus?

WHAT MAKES JESUS DIFFERENT from founders of other religions, such as Muhammad and Buddha? The most significant thing that sets Jesus apart from all others is his relationship with God the Father.
Read Colossians 1:15–20 and place a check mark by the characteristics that either describe Jesus or the Father or both.

	DESCRIBES JESUS	DESCRIBES THE FATHER
Invisible	_____	_____
Firstborn	_____	_____
Created All Things	_____	_____
All Things Created for Himself	_____	_____
Existed Before Anything Was Created	_____	_____
Holds All of Creation Together	_____	_____
Head of the Church	_____	_____
Supreme Over All Things	_____	_____
Fully Divine	_____	_____
Reconciles Man to Himself	_____	_____

• *What conclusions can you draw about Jesus and the Father sharing some of the above characteristics?*

• *Do you think there are any connections between God and Jesus concerning the characteristics they do not share?*

If so, what are those connections?

BEFORE *and* AFTER

Television commercials often use before-and-after pictures to portray the effectiveness of a product. Paul has done the same thing in Colossians 1:21–23. Read those verses and write down the words that Paul uses to describe us before and after Jesus' ministry on earth.

BEFORE   AFTER

DIGGING DEEPER

In light of this before-and-after story, consider the following questions.

1. How would you define *reconciliation* in today's language?

2. What does it mean to be "holy"?

3. How has Jesus Christ reconciled us?

4. What condition does Paul set forth (v. 23) for people to receive what Christ offers?

Under Construction

With Jesus in our lives, we are like a building that was run-down but now is being restored to its original grandeur. Through the power and supremacy of Jesus Christ, all the old rotten parts of our lives are being replaced with new and lasting parts. This restoration is not yet complete. Therefore, we are in a very real sense people who are under construction by the master carpenter, Jesus Christ.

Take a few moments to consider at least three areas where you have seen Jesus' power and supremacy in your life.

1.

2.

3.

Take a few moments to consider what changes or reemphases you need in your life because Jesus is more than a man—he is God. What things in these areas of your life have you not submitted to Jesus Christ's authority?

Your Home Life:

Your Marketplace:

Your Church:

Your Recreation Time:

Small Group Discussion

CONSIDERING SCRIPTURE
John 10:22–33
1. What do you think is the main reason that Jesus' claim to be God is offensive to some people?
   - a. They have a religious heritage that pictures God as one person.
   - b. They think any talk about being one with God is presumptuous.
   - c. There was a law in Judaism against claiming to be God, which was punishable by death.
   - d. They assume he was only a teacher and so was elevating himself.

2. Why do you think many people fail to realize or recognize that Jesus is God?
   - a. It's hard to imagine a man being God.
   - b. It's hard to imagine God being a man.
   - c. Why would God limit himself to a man's body?
   - d. It's hard to grasp why God would need to take such a drastic action to deal with sin.

3. How do you feel about Jesus declaring himself as our "shepherd" and making the statement that his sheep hear his voice, he knows them, and they follow him?
   - a. That sounds like a caring leader waiting to provide support as needed.
   - b. Knowing his voice in the crowd must be difficult sometimes.
   - c. It's easier to rest knowing that a caring shepherd is watching over us.
   - d. The gift of eternal life becomes more real to me, knowing our Shepherd lays down his life for his sheep.

1 John 5:1–20
4. What do you think is the most understandable benefit to being born of God?
   - a. Being a descendant within the blood line
   - b. Having God as our Father
   - c. Being a child in line for an inheritance
   - d. Depending on nurturing care and support
   - e. Receiving both sibling (including older brother) and family love

5. How do you think people "overcome" the world?
   - a. They are born again by the spirit of God to live a new life.
   - b. They are renewed and strengthened by the Spirit of God as a result of their faith.
   - c. They are identified as people who believe that Jesus is the Son of God.
   - d. They posture themselves for battle, hopeful for victory, all because of their position in Christ.

6. What aspect of God's promise of eternal life would you say gives the greatest assurance and certainty?
   - a. The clear record of testimony from God
   - b. The totally benevolent gift of eternal life that God has given the world
   - c. The qualifier that those who have the Son have absolute assurance of eternal life
   - d. The promise that this is for any who will establish their faith in Jesus alone

7. Which side benefit of eternal life do you find most comforting?
   - a. The promise of answered prayer (vv. 14, 15)
   - b. The continuing forgiveness of sin (vv. 16, 17)
   - c. The protection and deliverance from sin and evil (vv. 18, 19)
   - d. The additional gift of understanding and courage (v. 20)

TAKING THE NEXT STEP
John 20:31
8. What is the most significant way that Jesus' relationship with God bolsters your relationship with God?
   - a. He desires that I receive his authority into my life, providing direction for the future in all things.
   - b. He went before me and opened the door so I could enter and have a relationship with God. His death in my place paved the way.
   - c. He has provided a model for living in a close relationship with God.
   - d. He continues to provide assistance with my relationship by providing an indwelling presence of God through the Holy Spirit.

9. Since the purpose of the Bible is to lead us to faith in Jesus as the Christ and Son of God, what is the first thing you need to do to build up such a faith?
   - a. Read the Bible regularly
   - b. Talk with God in prayer more often
   - c. Start treating people more fairly
   - d. Repent of an ongoing sin
   - e. Allow the Holy Spirit, rather than my own will, to lead me
   - f. Worship God in private and public
   - g. Share my faith with others who don't know him
   - h. Turn my life over to Jesus
   - i. Other

Who do *you* **think** was more

P O W E R F U L,

Samantha of "Bewitched" or

Jeannie of "I Dream of Jeannie,"

and why do *you* **think** so?

VOTING TALLY

Samantha:

Jeannie:

Fundamental #6

We Are Saved by Grace, Through Faith, in Baptism

*T*he gospel of Jesus Christ must include not only an explanation of Christ's work and the salvation brought about by that work; it must also include instruction on how sinners may access this salvation. Without such instruction, the work of Christ would be in vain.

As an illustration, I have a friend with heart trouble who once told me he was taking ten kinds of medicine. I picture his physician telling him he can be cured if he just takes the right pills. The physician then gives him ten prescriptions. My friend takes them to a pharmacist, who takes ten large bottles of pills from his shelf and dumps about fifty of each into a large paper bag. He shakes them up and hands the bag to my friend, with no instructions as to how many of which pills to take how often! But without such instructions, my sick friend may as well have no medicine at all.

The fact is that the basic instruction on how to be saved is one of the essentials of the Christian faith. Unfortunately this point was not included in the early twentieth-century list of fundamentals. It is abundantly set forth, however, in the earliest gospel preaching recorded in the book of Acts and in the New Testament as a whole. When we examine this data we find that a sinner is saved *by grace, through faith, in baptism.*

—Jack Cottrell, *Faith's Fundamentals*

Central Theme	We are saved by grace, through faith, in baptism.
Lesson Aim	The learner will: • Be able to explain how grace, faith, and baptism work in our salvation • Be able to share in word pictures how God saves us
Bible Background	Romans 3:21–26; 6:1–4
For Further Study	Read Chapter Six of *Faith's Fundamentals*.

Classes

BUILDING COMMUNITY

Display <u>Transparency 6A</u>, and read to class members the following fictional story, which has been adapted from *Faith's Fundamentals.*

> Harvey has heart trouble. His doctor tells him he can be cured if he will take ten different kinds of pills. The doctor writes Harvey the ten prescriptions. Harvey takes the prescriptions to his pharmacist who takes ten large bottles of pills from his shelf and dumps about fifty of each into a large paper bag. He shakes them up and hands the bag to Harvey. The bag does not have any instructions as to how many of which pills to take or how often. Harvey buys the pills and takes them home, but he is uncertain how to take the medication that could save his life.

Discuss these questions with the class:
- What do you think Harvey should do?
- How would you feel if someone gave you medicine that would save you, but did not tell you how much and how often to take it?
- How do you think this story about Harvey relates to our receiving salvation from God?

Conclude the "Building Community" exercise by sharing these thoughts: **As important as it is to know how much medication to take when we are sick, it is even more important to know about salvation as sinners.** In *Faith's Fundamentals*, Jack Cottrell writes about the importance of knowing not only about salvation, but how to receive it. He writes,

> The gospel of Jesus Christ must include not only an explanation of Christ's work and the salvation brought about by that work; it must also include instruction on how sinners may access this salvation. Without such instruction, the work of Christ would be in vain. . . .
>   The fact is that the basic instruction on how to be saved is one of the essentials of the Christian faith. Unfortunately, this point was not included in the early twentieth-century list of fundamentals. It is abundantly set forth,

Getting to the Heart of It
8 Minutes

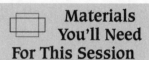

Materials You'll Need For This Session

Resource Sheets 6A, 6B, and Transparency 6A

Mini-lecture
2 Minutes

however, in the earliest gospel preaching recorded in the book of Acts and in the New Testament as a whole. When we examine this data we find that a sinner is saved *by grace, through faith, in baptism.*

CONSIDERING SCRIPTURE

How Are We Saved?
30 Minutes

Ask class members to work in groups of five to seven people as they look at Scripture to see how grace, faith, and baptism work in our salvation. Once the class is in their groups, hand out Resource Sheet 6A. Instruct the groups to pick two of the three headings to study. Tell them you want to make sure all three headings will be studied because you will ask them to share with the rest of the class what they have written. Therefore, you may need to ask one group to study an area other groups did not pick. The groups can spend about ten minutes on each of their two areas of study.

After the groups have taken twenty minutes to work on their assignments, ask them to share with the class what they have written. Below are the study questions and excerpts from *Faith's Fundamentals* to help direct the class discussion.

How Grace Works in Our Salvation

Study the following passages and write a paragraph that restates what these passages say about grace: Romans 3:23, 24; 5:20, 21; 11:5, 6; Ephesians 2:8; 2 Timothy 1:8, 9.

"Though we have sinned, God wants us back! He seeks us, pleads with us, begs us with outstretched arms to return to him."

"The gospel call, the call of grace, is God's simple plea: 'Turn! Turn away from sin, and return to me.'"

"Grace calls the sinner not only to turn *away* from sin but also to turn *toward* God and his Kingdom of Love and Light . . . Hearing the call of grace, the sinner turns and calls upon the gracious God to receive him and bestow the promised salvation. The call of grace is not to be regarded as a legalistic demand, but as a gracious opportunity."

"Scripture speaks of repentance as something God grants both to Israel and the Gentiles."

How Faith Works in Our Salvation

Study the following passages and write a paragraph that restates what these passages say about how faith works in our salvation: Acts 26:17, 18; Romans 4:1–8; 1 Corinthians 2:4, 5; Ephesians 6:16; 2 Timothy 4:7.

"What leads a sinner to turn to the Lord, that is, to repent and call on his name? The answer is *faith.*"

"Faith in God's Word—both his law and his gospel—is thus a necessary means of receiving the content of saving grace."

"Faith is first of all *assenting* to the truth of certain statements, such as the "essentials": believing *that* God exists (Hebrews 11:6), believing *that* Jesus rose from the dead (Romans 10:9), and the rest."

"Faith is also *trusting* a person enough to take him at his word and to rely on him."

How Baptism Works in Our Salvation

Study the following passages and write a paragraph that restates what these passages say concerning how baptism works in our salvation: Galatians 3:27–29; Colossians 2:11, 12; Mark 16:16; Acts 2:38; Romans 6:3, 4; 1 Peter 3:18–21.

"What is Christian baptism? It is *immersion.* Something is baptized when it is dipped or immersed into water or some other liquid. . . .

[Baptism] is the immersion of a *believer* in water. A person not old enough to consciously turn to God in repentance and faith does not *need* baptism and receives no benefit from being immersed into water. Immersion is for those old enough to understand their condition as guilty sinners under the condemnation of the law, and old enough to understand and accept the gospel message of salvation through Jesus Christ."

"All this [grace, faith, baptism] together is the essential gospel. We cannot leave any of it out. Most of Christendom will agree with this, up to the very last point—about Christian baptism. But on this point, as all others, I would rather agree with Peter and Paul and Philip and God himself than the whole Christian world (Romans 3:4). It was good for Paul and Philip, and it's good enough for me."

TAKING THE NEXT STEP

Hand out copies of Resource Sheet 6B to class members. Read through the directions on the resource sheet with the class. Then challenge the class to think not only of a word picture they could share with an unsaved friend or new Christian, but one that would at the same time illustrate their life in Christ. Listed on the following page are ideas for word pictures you can use to help illustrate this exercise to the class.

Word Pictures
20 Minutes

Grace
• Grace is like receiving a *pardon* from the governor for a crime.
• Grace is like someone buying you a *lottery ticket* and the ticket winning.

Faith
• Faith is like holding onto a *rope* dangling from a cliff.
• Faith is like a *ship* that will take you across water that can only be crossed by boat.

Baptism
• Baptism is like taking a *bath* that cleans all the dirt from your body.
• Baptism is like *dry cleaning* clothes. The dry cleaning is something someone else does for you.

After the class has had about fifteen minutes to illustrate their word pictures, ask volunteers to share their word pictures with the class. Once those who want to share have done so, or as class time expires, take a few moments to close the class in prayer, thanking God for not only providing salvation, but also for showing us clearly how we gain access to salvation by grace, through faith, in baptism. Pray also for opportunities to share with a friend who does not know Jesus Christ.

PLAN TWO

Groups

BUILDING COMMUNITY

What gift that you received as a child was the biggest surprise?
* How old were you?
* What was the occasion?

CONSIDERING SCRIPTURE

Hand out copies of <u>Resource Sheet 6C</u>. For each of the three sections, read the corresponding Scriptures and then discuss the questions that follow.

TAKING THE NEXT STEP

Ask participants to pair up with each other. (This may work best if married couples are not partners. It may also help for men to pair up with men and women with women, if possible.) Ask the pairs to discuss one or both of the sets of questions under "Taking the Next Step" on Resource Sheet 6C. (You may pick the question for them or allow each pair to choose which one they want to discuss.)

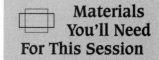
Materials You'll Need For This Session

Resource Sheet 6C

OPTION
Accountability Partners
Have accountability partners do the "Taking the Next Step" activity from Resource Sheet 6C. (See instructions at left.)

OPTION
Memory Verse
"For it is by grace you have been saved, through faith—and this not from yourselves, it is the gift of God" (Ephesians 2:8).

SAVED

By Grace
In Faith
Through Baptism

How Grace Works in Our Salvation

Study the following passages and write a paragraph that restates in your own words what these passages say about how grace works in our salvation: Romans 3:23, 24; 5:20, 21; 11:5, 6; Ephesians 2:8; 2 Timothy 1:8, 9.

How Faith Works in Our Salvation

Study the following passages and write a paragraph that restates in your own words what these passages say about how faith works in our salvation: Acts 26:17, 18; Romans 4:1–8; 1 Corinthians 2:4, 5; Ephesians 6:16; 2 Timothy 4:7.

How Baptism Works in Our Salvation

Study the following passages and write a paragraph that restates in your own words what these passages say about how baptism works in our salvation: Galatians 3:27–29; Colossians 2:11, 12; Mark 16:16; Acts 2:38; Romans 6:3, 4; 1 Peter 3:18–21.

A Picture Is Worth
a Thousand Words

A picture is worth a thousand words. Even though you have written in words how grace, faith, and baptism work in our salvation, communicating those things to someone who does not know Jesus Christ may not be completely understood. This is when a word picture can help communicate an idea when mere words may not be enough.

Think of a word picture you could use in a conversation with a friend that would illustrate one of the three ways we access salvation: grace, faith, baptism. Draw your word picture below, and write any explanations that describe in detail how you see your picture illustrating grace, faith, or baptism.

Small Group Discussion

CONSIDERING SCRIPTURE

Ephesians 2:1–10 (We Are Saved by Grace . . .)

1. Which phrase *best* describes your pre-Christian life?
   a. Dead in my sins
   b. In a trance—following the ways of the world
   c. Addicted—gratifying the cravings of my sinful nature
   d. Near death and pretty hopeless

2. With which one of the following verses could you best describe God's grace to you?
   a. 2 Corinthians 12:9—God's grace is sufficient and made perfect in my weakness.
   b. Ephesians 1:7—Through God's grace I have redemption and the forgiveness of sin.
   c. James 4:6—The Lord gives me more grace when I am humble.
   d. 1 Timothy 1:14—Grace has been poured out on me abundantly, along with faith and love.

3. Which of the following verses best describes why you think you did not deserve God's grace, mercy, and riches before conversion?
   a. Romans 5:6–10—I was an enemy of God.
   b. Colossians 3:5–10—My earthly nature was in opposition to God.
   c. Philippians 3:17–21—My mind was on earthly things.
   d. 2 Timothy 3:2–4—My life was full of sin.

Romans 3:21–26 (Through Faith . . .)

4. Which attitude do you think most prevents people from accepting God's forgiveness by faith in Christ alone?
   a. A mistrust in the Bible
   b. A misunderstanding about Christian baptism
   c. A feeling that we must have to do something to pay for that kind of complete forgiveness
   d. A sense of I-can-do-it-myself pride

5. Which of these responses to God's grace have you experienced? (Check as many as apply.)
   ❏ I felt a serious desire to get right with God.
   ❏ I repented of my sins.
   ❏ I agreed that Jesus came to die in my place.
   ❏ I prayed and asked God to forgive my sins, and I gave myself to him totally and willingly.
   ❏ I proclaimed my belief in Jesus' all sufficient death in my place and committed myself to his sovereign authority over me in public.
   ❏ I allowed myself to be baptized to finish the transition from old life to new life.
   ❏ I've begun the journey of maturity in Christ.

Romans 6:1–4 (In Baptism)

6. With God's help, how do you need to strengthen your Christian walk right now?
   a. Replace selfish and prideful attitudes with an attitude of humility and gratefulness for all God has done
   b. Begin correcting severed relationships and ask forgiveness of those who have been offended
   c. Commit my time, talent, and treasure fully to the Lord for his supervision and direction
   d. Seek a place of fellowship—getting involved where there is both small groups and meaningful large-group events

7. What symbolic part of Christian baptism means the most to you?
   a. The death, burial, and resurrection of a life (Romans 6:2–4)
   b. The remission of sin and the gift of the Holy Spirit (Acts 2:38)
   c. Being clothed with Christ (Galatians 3:27)
   d. "Not the removal of dirt from the body but the pledge of a good conscience toward God" (1 Peter 3:21)

TAKING THE NEXT STEP

8. Did any part of this Bible study raise questions in your mind about the certainty of your salvation?

   • Which verses from this Bible study make you feel acceptable to God?

   • Pray together, thanking God for his gift of grace.

9. List below names of people you know who have not yet accepted God's grace.

Neighbors:

Friends:

Co-workers:

Family:

Church Visitors:

Other:

   • Talk briefly about one or two people on the lists with whom you might have an opportunity to share God's grace.

   • Pray for these people and for one another.

Harvey & His Heart

Harvey has heart trouble. His doctor tells him he can be cured if he will take ten different kinds of pills. The doctor writes Harvey the ten prescriptions. Harvey takes the prescriptions to his pharmacist who takes ten large bottles of pills from his shelf and dumps about fifty of each into a large paper bag. He shakes them up and hands the bag to Harvey. The bag does not have any instructions as to how many of which pills to take or how often. Harvey buys the pills and takes them home, but he is uncertain how to take the medication that could save his life.

Fundamental #7

Jesus Is Coming Again

*F*ew doctrines have divided Bible believers more than eschatology [the doctrine about the end times]. Disagreements abound on practically every detail. Nevertheless there is one central belief on which they all agree: *Jesus is coming again.* This has always been one of the fundamentals or essentials. . . .

The Bible says human history had a distinct beginning when God created the heavens and the earth (Genesis 1:1). His goal was a race of freewill creatures who would voluntarily glorify him and gratefully enjoy his blessings forever.

Progress toward this goal was interrupted almost at once by the fall of Adam and Eve into sin. As a result, the earth and the whole human race came under the control of sin and death (Romans 5:12 ff.; 8:18 ff.). But this did not defeat God's purpose. He will achieve his goal by an alternate route—the way of salvation through Jesus Christ. Through his cross and resurrection, Jesus redeems and restores the creation, setting it on its current trajectory toward the original goal.

So cosmic history as we know it will end when God decides his goal has been reached. The climactic event that will accomplish this closure is the second coming of Jesus.

—Jack Cottrell, *Faith's Fundamentals*

Central Theme	Believing in Jesus' physical return is essential for being his disciple.
Lesson Aim	The student will: • Be able to state why Christ's physical return is essential • Be able to set a personal plan of readiness for Christ's return
Bible Background	Matthew 24:36–44
For Further Study	Read Chapter Seven of *Faith's Fundamentals*.

Classes

BUILDING COMMUNITY

Display Transparency 7A. Cover the bottom half with a piece of paper so the class can only see the top question. Ask the class to respond after you read the question aloud: **If Jesus were to return tomorrow at 8 P.M., assuming you didn't know about it in advance, what would you be doing?**

After the class has taken time to respond to the first question, remove the piece of paper covering the bottom question. Ask the class to respond: **If you knew in advance that Jesus was returning tomorrow at 8 P.M., what would you be doing?** As students share their answers, help them begin to think about how Christ's imminent return should change the way they live each day.

Hand out copies of Resource Sheet 7A to the class. Once everyone has a resource sheet, ask students to work together with partners to complete the sheet. They have five to six minutes to complete this exercise. After the time is up, ask the class to come back together to review their answers. Use this activity strictly for building community and fun. Use it to start the class thinking about Jesus' return. Avoid getting into a discussion about what views the class should hold concerning the end times.

Here are the answers to Resource Sheet 7A: (1) b; (2) h; (3) k; (4) a; (5) f; (6) l; (7) d; (8) e; (9) j; (10) o

CONSIDERING SCRIPTURE

There are many questions people have about this time in the history of the world. Not all the questions need answers, but some issues are important. This session will focus on issues vital to you as it relates to Christ's second coming.

Divide the class into groups of five to seven each and distribute Resource Sheet 7B. Ask the class to follow the instructions on the sheet. After the class has taken about fifteen minutes to complete the study, take five minutes to review their answers and comments.

After reviewing the groups' answers to the Bible study, take a few moments to discuss the importance of this doctrine of Christ's return.

Two Questions
10 Minutes

OPTION
The Final Exam
10 Minutes

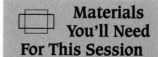

Materials You'll Need For This Session

Resource Sheets 7A–7C, pens or pencils, Transparencies 7A and 7B

Small Groups Discussion
20 Minutes

Mini-lecture
10 Minutes

Display Transparency 7B. **Jack Cottrell has given us three reasons he believes this doctrine is one of the essentials of the Christian faith. He does not believe that a person can deny the second coming and still be a Christian. In *Faith's Fundamentals* he states why.** Stated below are the three reasons, which are are also on Transparency 7B, with the addition of explanations for each reason to share with the class.

1. To vindicate God, his purpose, and his plan

"Ever since the beginning (Genesis 3:15), God has been promising redemption and eternal life for believers and vengeance upon his enemies. Will it ever happen? Is it all a delusion and a false hope? Are we as Christians wasting our time and energy 'living for Jesus'?"

2. To uphold the integrity of God's physical creation

"In nonbiblical worldviews, the physical universe is either an accident or a mistake. But according to the Bible, it is the deliberate creation of God and thus is part of his purpose for mankind. The tragedy is that sin has perverted and corrupted not just human life but the whole universe (Romans 8:18–23).

"Those who believe the world originated through purely natural processes (such as a mysterious 'big bang') believe it will continue to operate according to those processes until it eventually runs down and enters a state of universal, permanent inertia. The world will then be one big cosmic junk pile. Many Christians have been influenced by this and other pagan worldviews, and have come to think of the universe as just a temporary stage in human development, something that will be discarded when we advance on to 'heaven.'"

3. To guarantee the accountability of man

"God created us with free will, but how can we be held accountable for our choices? The answer is the final judgment. When Jesus comes again, one of his main purposes will be to bring every responsible person into judgment."

TAKING THE NEXT STEP

Reality Check
20 Minutes

Distribute copies of Resource Sheet 7C. Ask students to find a partner with whom to work. Ask someone to read the opening paragraphs aloud to the class. Then encourage students to spend about ten minutes reflecting on the questions below the opening paragraphs. Once time has been given to work quietly on the questions, have the partners share with each other some of the things they need to change and what they plan to make a priority in their lives. Then have them pray for one another that God will help them focus on what is really important in light of Christ's imminent return.

PLAN TWO

Groups

BUILDING COMMUNITY

Suppose an angel appeared to you and told you Jesus will return in exactly one week. You're the only one who knows and you're not allowed to tell anyone else. What will you do during the next week?

CONSIDERING SCRIPTURE

Distribute copies of Resource Sheet 7D to the group. For each of the three sections, read the corresponding Scripture verses and then discuss the questions that follow.

TAKING THE NEXT STEP

Discuss questions 10 and 11 on the resource sheet and then close the session in prayer.

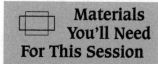

Materials You'll Need For This Session

Resource Sheet 7D

OPTION
Accountability Partners
Ask accountability partners to meet to discuss how this series has helped them grow in knowledge and spirit. How will these fundamentals of their faith affect the way they live on a day-to-day basis until Christ returns?

OPTION
Memory Verse
"The Lord is not slow in keeping his promise, as some understand slowness. He is patient with you, not wanting anyone to perish, but everyone to come to repentance" (2 Peter 3:9).

The FINAL Exam

This session focuses on the second coming of Christ. Take a few moments to test your knowledge of the end times. One correct meaning for each term is given below. Write the letter that you believe is the correct response on the line provided in the left column.

1. _____ Eschatology

2. _____ 666

3. _____ Armageddon

4. _____ The Rapture

5. _____ The Antichrist

6. _____ Parousia

7. _____ The Book of Life

8. _____ The Seventh Seal

9. _____ The Tribulation

10. _____ Millennium

a. To be physically snatched away at Christ's return

b. The study of last things

c. A best-seller by Stephen King

d. A list of those who have been saved

e. What will be broken to reveal last-day events

f. The prince of Christ's enemies

g. To be able to sing rap songs well

h. The mark of the beast

j. A period of persecution

k. The last and great battle

l. A Greek word used to describe Christ's abiding physical presence when he returns

m. A Greek word that means "revelation"

n. The star seal in a circus act

o. The thousand-year reign of God's kingdom on earth

p. A Greek word that means "judgment"

What Will the
END OF THE WORLD
Look Like?

Read Matthew 24:36–44. Based on this passage of Scripture, answer the following questions about the end times and what they will look like.

1. What will the time before Jesus' return be like?

2. What will Jesus' return be like?

3. What will happen after Jesus' return?

4. Why is Jesus' return necessary? (Also refer to Acts 3:21 and 2 Peter 3:3–10.)

Reality Check

We can become complacent about life's day-in and day-out routines and habits. Those routines and habits reflect what is really important to us. However, when adversity or trauma come into our lives, many of those routines and habits are put into perspective. What earlier seemed important is no longer vital. Moments like those can be "reality checks." Often we find that some of the things we know are most important are the things we have not paid attention to.

Looking forward to Christ's return is one of those things that is of utmost importance to Christians. God is giving us time to make preparation, but do our lives really reflect a readiness for Jesus' return?

✔   ✔   ✔   ✔   ✔   ✔   ✔

Knowing that Jesus is coming back, what must you change in your life to prepare for his return?

Determine what is really important in your life. List three or four things in order of priority. Then lay out action steps for working toward accomplishing them.

O

O

O

O

Small Group Discussion

CONSIDERING SCRIPTURE
Matthew 24:36–44

1. What is the most important thing you can do to prepare for Christ's return, whether it's tomorrow or after your lifetime on earth?
   - a. Put my faith and trust in Jesus as both Savior and Lord
   - b. Speak to family and friends about the change in my life brought by a full commitment to Jesus
   - c. Live daily with an expectant attitude
   - d. Boldly assert my faith as much as possible with those who are lost

2. Jesus compared the last days to the days of Noah, before the great flood. Which of these similarities motivates you the most to be prepared for Christ's return?
   - a. Just as then, there has been plenty of time to get ready.
   - b. Most people are living life unaware that Jesus is coming back.
   - c. Like then, if it happened today, more would be lost than saved.
   - d. Like then, God has a plan, and he has told us about it.

Matthew 24:45–51

3. Which aspect of the story about the faithful and wise servant helps you the most in being prepared for Jesus' return?
   - a. Responsible stewardship: Using my gifts, abilities, and assignment faithfully until the Lord returns.
   - b. Certainty of judgment: It will be certain and terrible if one is unfaithful.
   - c. Responsibility for serving others: Serving is the most identifiable quality of a faithful steward.
   - d. Responsibility for witnessing to others: The fellow servants will do as they see fit unless the steward gives directions and sounds the warning.

4. Our Master does indeed seem to be "staying away a long time." What do you need to start doing to remain a faithful servant in the meantime? (Check all that apply.)
   - ❑ Spend more time communicating with God through Bible study and prayer
   - ❑ Spend more time with other Christians, giving and receiving support and encouragement
   - ❑ Spend more time serving others
   - ❑ Spend more time sharing my faith with others
   - ❑ Get to know Jesus as my Savior and Master
   - ❑ Get rid of a sinful or addictive habit or lifestyle
   - ❑ Learn to forgive people who have hurt me
   - ❑ Receive forgiveness from others

2 Peter 3:3–14

5. Scoffers are to have an important role in the last days. How do you think their attitudes will affect people?
   - a. Their questions about what's taking the Lord so long may cause some believers to doubt.
   - b. Their mocking will motivate the church to pray and serve more faithfully.
   - c. Their lack of memory that God spoke the world into existence will prevent them from understanding the timing of the Lord, especially that he is not in a hurry.
   - d. People will not recall that the warning of God took 120 years before he flooded the world and that most people were unaware of what was happening.

6. How does knowing that the earth will someday be destroyed change your outlook on life?
   - a. Everything I've spent my life doing is only temporary.
   - b. My life could be more meaningful if everyday I asked, "Is what I'm doing today of eternal significance?"
   - c. An eternal view could help me see clearly that lost people matter to God.
   - d. Relationships would be a priority over tasks in my daily planner.

7. "We are looking forward to a new heaven and a new earth, the house of righteousness" (v. 13). What hope does that give you?
   - a. The world with its impurities will be changed.
   - b. The effects of ungodliness and sin will be removed form the earth.
   - c. No more pollution!
   - d. God's new creation will look and be more wonderful than anything seen before.

8. What most prohibits you from staying focused on the new heaven and new earth?
   - a. The present is more urgent than the future.
   - b. The "stuff of life" strongly supports a self-centered view of time and the world.
   - c. The tasks I am pursuing (work, home, and even church) consume my thinking.
   - d. My sin and its consequences sidetrack me from the things of the Lord.

continued on next page

9. How could God's waiting to return be to your advantage?

    a. I have time to encourage a godly partner.

    b. I have time to raise God-fearing children.

    c. I am able to spend time encouraging others to receive Christ.

    d. I have had an opportunity to hear the gospel and commit myself to Christ.

    e. I have time to develop a stronger relationship with God.

TAKING THE NEXT STEP

10. Peter says we need to live holy and godly lives as we expect the second coming. What is the first thing you need to do to start living a holy and godly life?

    a. Start my days with a time of prayer and a word from the Lord

    b. Guard my heart and mind from sinful situations

    c. View my relationships as situations in which I am an ambassador for Christ

    d. Schedule my time so that my work is "as unto the Lord"

11. What is one specific way you can reflect an attitude of expectancy for Jesus' return?

    a. Mark time in my daily planner to pray for lost co-workers, friends, family members, and acquaintances

    b. Plan time in my weekly schedule to challenge unbelievers or seekers to respond to Christ

    c. Insure that I do not neglect meeting together to encourage my brothers and sisters to remain faithful—particularly as we see the last day getting nearer (cf. Hebrews 10:25)

    d. Other

If Jesus were to return tomorrow at 8 P.M., assuming you didn't know about it in advance, what would you be doing?

If you knew in advance that Jesus was returning tomorrow at 8 P.M., what would you be doing?

3
REASONS WHY
CHRIST'S RETURN IS NECESSARY

---

1. To vindicate God, his purpose, and his plan

2. To uphold the integrity of God's physical creation

3. To guarantee the accountability of man

OTHER CREATIVE GROUPS GUIDES
from Standard Publishing

A CALL TO PRAYER

Guide by Jan Johnson
Learn to pray more effectively, more sincerely, with more power, and without hindrances. Class or group members will gain practical knowledge about why they should pray, how to pray, and what to pray for. Start a prayer revival in your congregation!
Order number 11-40309 *(ISBN 0-7847-0309-4)*

CLAIMING YOUR PLACE

Guide by Michael C. Mack and Mark A. Taylor
Help your small group or class learn how to find where they fit into the life of the church. Seven sessions will guide your group to greater commitment and involvement in the body. They'll find a place of faith, service, bold witness, passion, and more.
Order number 11-40305 *(ISBN 0-7847-0285-3)*

HEARING GOD

Guide by Michael C. Mack and Mark A. Taylor
Help your group or class learn how to read God's Word—and really understand it! In just six lessons, you will demonstrate eight simple steps that can make anyone feel at home in the Bible and be able to put it into practice.
Order number 11-40306 *(ISBN 0-7847-0286-1)*

FIND US FAITHFUL

Guide by Michael D. McCann
Help your group members learn to pass on their faith to the next generation, to their children and to others in their spheres of influence. Christianity is always one generation from extinction, so it is critical that we learn how to pass on our faith.
Order number 11-40308 *(ISBN 0-7847-0308-6)*

To order, contact your local Christian bookstore.
(If the book is out of stock, you can order by calling 1-800-543-1353.)

STANDARD
PUBLISHING
Cincinnati, Ohio